COZY KNITS

Inspiring | Educating | Creating | Entertaining

Brimming with creative inspiration, how-to projects, and useful information to enrich your everyday life, Quarto Knows is a favorite destination for those pursuing their interests and passions. Visit our site and dig deeper with our books into your area of interest: Quarto Creates, Quarto Cooks, Quarto Homes, Quarto Lives, Quarto Drives, Quarto Explores, Quarto Gifts, or Quarto Kids.

First Published in 2021 by Voyageur Press, an imprint of The Quarto Group, 100 Cummings Center, Suite 265-D, Beverly, MA 01915, USA.
T (978) 282-9590 F (978) 283-2742 QuartoKnows.com

Voyageur Press titles are also available at discount for retail, wholesale, promotional, and bulk purchase. For details, contact the Special Sales Manager by email at specialsales@quarto.com or by mail at The Quarto Group, Attn: Special Sales Manager, 100 Cummings Center, Suite 265-D, Beverly, MA 01915, USA.

25 24 23 22 21   1 2 3 4 5

ISBN: 978-0-7603-7353-8

Digital edition published in 2021
eISBN: 978-0-7603-7354-5

Library of Congress Cataloging-in-Publication Data

Names: Flanders, Sue, 1960- author. | Kosel, Janine, 1964- author.
Title: Cozy knits : 30 hat, mitten, scarf and sock projects from around the
    world/ Sue Flanders & Janine Kosel.
Description: Beverly, MA : Voyageur Press, 2022. | Includes index. |
    Summary: "Cozy Knits presents 50 of the coziest, globally-inspired
    patterns for hats, mittens, and gloves-including stylish traditional
    projects from Scandinavia, Eastern Europe, the British Isles, the
    Americas, and Asia"-- Provided by publisher.
Identifiers: LCCN 2021045479 (print) | LCCN 2021045480 (ebook) | ISBN
    9780760373538 (trade paperback) | ISBN 9780760373545 (ebook)
Subjects: LCSH: Knitting--Patterns. | Hats. | Mittens. | Scarves. | Socks.
Classification: LCC TT825 .F5558 2022 (print) | LCC TT825 (ebook) | DDC
    746.43/2--dc23
LC record available at https://lccn.loc.gov/2021045479
LC ebook record available at https://lccn.loc.gov/2021045480

Design: Ashley Prine, Tandem Books
Cover Image: rau+barber
Page Layout: Ashley Prine, Tandem Books
Photography: Sue Flanders and Janine Kosel; model photography: 83, 97, 88, 99, 104,114 by rau+barber
Image Credits: yarn icon © AVIcon/Shutterstock; 5,9,65,123 © rraya/Shutterstock

Printed in China

COZY KNITS

30 Hat, Mitten, Scarf, and Sock Projects from Around the World

Kari Cornell, Editor

VOYAGEUR PRESS

CONTENTS

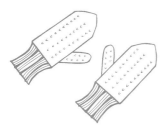

Introduction

By Nancy Bush

True or classic knitting is believed to have its origins in the Middle East, likely in Islamic Egypt. One of the oldest known pieces of true knitting was found in what is now Cairo. It has sadly been lost, but was documented, along with an image in *Mary Thomas's Knitting Book* (1938). The knitted piece was made of silk, in crossed stockinette stitch (where each stitch is twisted) at a gauge of about 36 stitches (15 cm) to an inch. As the piece was a fragment, it is impossible to know what the original item was.

The craft of knitting is believed to have made its way into southern Europe by the thirteenth century. We have two knitted cushions as evidence of this, placed in Spanish tombs around 1275 CE. These pieces are some of the earliest examples of knitting known in Europe. The ornate two-color patterning and fine gauge (20 stitches to 1 inch) offer evidence that they were made by a highly skilled craftsperson. The fine metal needles necessary for such intricate work was evidence of the skill of Spanish-Arab metalworkers.

It is only a short stretch of the imagination to realize that the wider population would adopt the same techniques. The skill of knitting spread due to several factors: Knitting could be done with a few handmade tools. Yarn was readily available, and spindle spinning was a known skill. The techniques of knitting were not difficult to learn and, perhaps most importantly, knitted fabric could be made in broad strips and sheets for scarves or to fit special shapes, like feet and fingers. Stockings, gloves, and hats needed to fit close to the body, required stretch in order to be put on, and offered protection from the elements. Because knitting was done with long lengths of spun fiber, it was quicker and easier than the older technique of needle looping and required fewer tools and less space than weaving. If a mistake was made, knitting was easily pulled out. For all of these reasons, knitting must have been considered the "wonder textile" of its day, and as such, became very popular, very quickly.

While some patterns didn't travel far from where they were invented, others traveled the world. Many ornate patterns found on knitted fabric are cross-cultural. A good example of this is the eight-pointed star, found on Turkish rugs and the Norwegian socks in this text. This pattern has traveled the world and, happily, suits knitting very well because it can be worked in a grid configuration.

This collection of cozy knits was inspired by traditions, places, and people from around the world. It is a cross-section of the many possibilities there can be for knitting a sock, a hat, a pair of mittens, a scarf, and more. There is interesting "architecture," structure, and construction; varied, bold, and charming decoration; and glimpses into traditions that shaped the ideas behind the designs and patterns. We hope you enjoy this trip around the world in cozy knits!

A Note About the Yarns in This Book

The yarns used throughout this book are listed in the materials section of each project. If you would like an alternate option for any yarn, or if a yarn has been discontinued, you can go to www.yarnsub.com to find options for substitution.

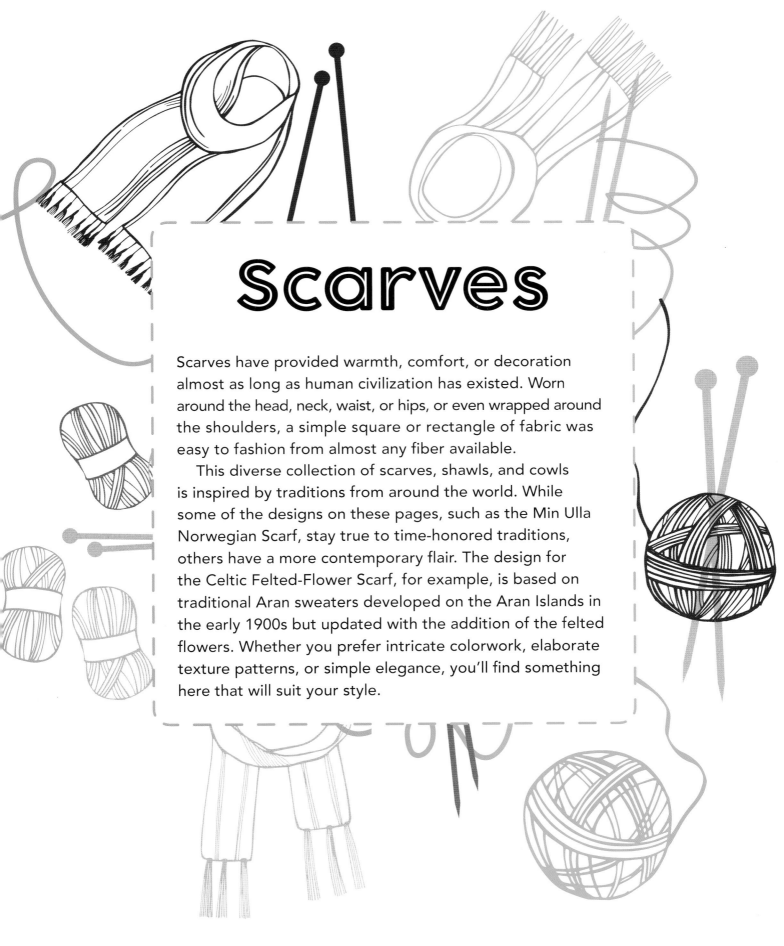

Scarves

Scarves have provided warmth, comfort, or decoration almost as long as human civilization has existed. Worn around the head, neck, waist, or hips, or even wrapped around the shoulders, a simple square or rectangle of fabric was easy to fashion from almost any fiber available.

This diverse collection of scarves, shawls, and cowls is inspired by traditions from around the world. While some of the designs on these pages, such as the Min Ulla Norwegian Scarf, stay true to time-honored traditions, others have a more contemporary flair. The design for the Celtic Felted-Flower Scarf, for example, is based on traditional Aran sweaters developed on the Aran Islands in the early 1900s but updated with the addition of the felted flowers. Whether you prefer intricate colorwork, elaborate texture patterns, or simple elegance, you'll find something here that will suit your style.

Min Ulla
Norwegian Scarf

Design by Elinor Brown

This Norwegian-style scarf is made in the round as a tube with its ends grafted together in the finishing process. Symmetrical from the center point, it is comprised of many very simple band repeats interspersed with a few more complicated snowflake motifs and larger XOXO patterns.

Finished Measurements
74¼" x 7½" [188.5 x 19cm]

Materials ◢4◣
Berroco *Ultra Alpaca* (worsted weight; 50% alpaca/50% wool; 219yds [200m] per 3½ oz [100g] skein): 3 skeins each Charcoal Mix #6289 (MC) and Winter White #6201 (CC)

Size 6 [4mm] 16" [40cm] circular needle or size needed to obtain gauge

Size G/6 [4mm] crochet hook (optional for provisional CO)

Spare needle

Waste yarn

Stitch markers

Tapestry needle

Gauge
26 sts and 26 rnds = 4" [10cm] in stranded 2-color St st.

Adjust needle size as necessary to obtain correct gauge.

Pattern Note
This scarf is worked in the round with both ends grafted to close the tube.

Special Technique
Provisional Cast-On: With a crochet hook and waste yarn, make a chain several sts longer than the desired CO. With a circular knitting needle and project yarn, pick up the indicated number of sts in the "bumps" on the back of the chain. When indicated in the pat, "unzip" the crochet chain to free the live sts.

Instructions

Leaving a 22" [56cm] tail and using MC, provisionally CO 96 sts; pm for beg of rnd and join, taking care not to twist sts.

Work Charts 1–6 in order.

You are now at the middle of the scarf.

Turn the charts upside down and work Charts 6–1 in reverse order (starting from what was the top row of each chart) so that the 2nd half mirrors the first half.

Cut the yarn, leaving a 22" [56cm] MC tail.

Finishing

Place the first 48 sts of the rnd on a spare needle, leaving the rem 48 sts on the working circular needle. Use the MC tail and Kitchener st to graft the sts tog.

Weave in all tails on the WS, turning the scarf inside out if necessary.

Unzip the provisional CO, placing the first 48 sts on a spare needle and the last 48 sts on the working circular needle. Use the MC tail and Kitchener st to graft the sts tog.

Wet-block the scarf to even out the color pattern.

COLOR KEY
■ MC
□ CC

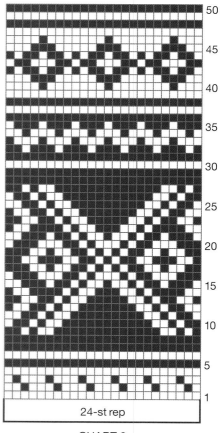

16-st rep

CHART 1

24-st rep

CHART 2

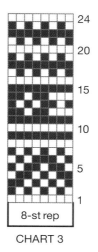

24
20
15
10
5
1

8-st rep

CHART 3

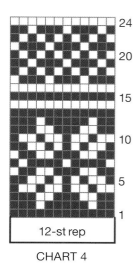

24
20
15
10
5
1

12-st rep

CHART 4

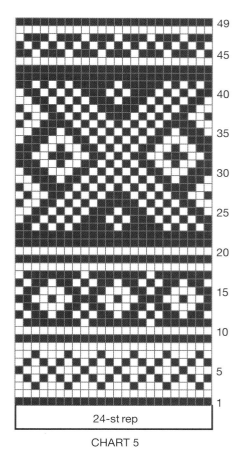

49
45
40
35
30
25
20
15
10
5
1

24-st rep

CHART 5

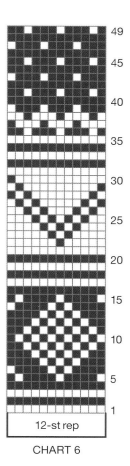

49
45
40
35
30
25
20
15
10
5
1

12-st rep

CHART 6

Icelandic Yoke Scarf

Design by Gretchen Funk

The Lopapeysa, or Icelandic Yoke Sweater, has a fairly recent history despite its traditional look. This scarf echoes the beautiful Icelandic yoke patterns, which decrease from the shoulders to the neck. Knitting with Icelandic unspun yarn is an amazing adventure. It is a fragile yarn, much like pencil roving. Once knit, however, it creates a strong, lofty, and amazingly warm fabric. If it breaks, overlap and rub the ends together and it will blend like magic! The yarn softens greatly with blocking.

Finished Measurements

Unblocked: 55" [139.5cm] long x 6" [15cm] wide at narrowest middle; 10½" [27cm] wide at ends.

Blocked: 65" [165cm] long x 5½" [14cm] wide at narrowest middle; 10" [25cm] wide at ends.

Materials 🧶2

Schoolhouse Press *UnSpun Icelandic* (sport weight; 100% Icelandic unspun wool; 300yds [274m] per 3½ oz [100g] wheel): 2 wheels Blacksheep (A); 1 wheel each Spruce (B) and Sage (C)

Size 8 [5mm] 16" [40cm] circular needle or 40" [100cm] circular needle for Magic Loop method

Spare needle

Size H/8 [5mm] crochet hook (optional for provisional CO)

Stitch marker

Tapestry needle

Gauge

16 sts and 17 rnds = 4" [10 cm] using yarn doubled in 2-color stranded St st, blocked.

Adjust needle size as necessary to obtain correct gauge.

Pattern Notes

This scarf is worked in the round in 2 pieces that are grafted together at the back neck. Unless you are using Judy's Magic Cast-On, the ends will also be grafted together.

Hold 2 strands of yarn together throughout. Use the inside and outside ends of the wheel.

If a strand of yarn breaks, simply overlap the ends and vigorously rub the 2 ends together between your hands to splice.

When grafting, twist the 2 strands together slightly to give them additional strength.

Use smaller needles if necessary in a single-color section to obtain the gauge.

Instructions

First Side

With 2 ends of MC and using Provisional Cast-On or Judy's Magic Cast-On, CO 80 sts; mark beg of rnd.

Knit 4 rnds.

Work 45 rnds following chart, decreasing as indicated and weaving in ends as you go—50 sts.

Knit 16" [40cm] in MC; the piece will measure approx 27½" [70cm].

Put work on waste yarn.

2nd Side

Work as for first side, leaving sts on needle.

Weave in all ends that are not already woven in.

Finishing

Using yarn doubled, graft the 2 sides together using Kitchener st.

If provisional CO was used, unzip the waste yarn and divide the sts evenly on 2 needles. Graft sts to close ends.

Block scarf to finished measurements.

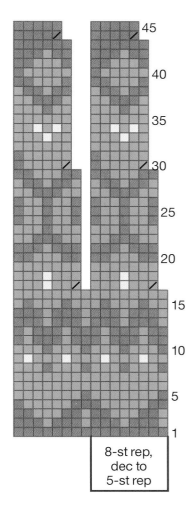

ICELANDIC YOKE CHART

8-st rep,
dec to
5-st rep

STITCH AND COLOR KEY

- ■ Knit with A
- ■ Knit with B
- □ Knit with C
- ◪ K2tog with B
- ◪ K2tog with A

Bavarian Twisted Stitches
Commuter Scarf

Design by Dawn Brocco

This scarf modernizes a traditional Bavarian twisted-stitch pattern by shaping the outside of the pattern, adding a curvaceous touch. I've also chosen to purl the rear stitch in the traveling pairs of stitches to give the twisted knit stitches on the surface even more relief.

Finished Measurements

Width: 2¾–4¼" [7–11cm]

Length: 67" [170cm], excluding tassels

Materials 🧶4🧶

Cascade Yarns *Eco Wool* (heavy worsted weight; 100% Peruvian wool; 478yds [437m] per 9oz [255g] hank): 1 hank Ecru #8010

Size 9 (5.5mm) needles or size needed to obtain gauge

Tapestry needle

Gauge

19 sts and 22 rows = 4" [10cm] in St st.

24 sts and 22 rows = 4" [10cm] in pat.

Adjust needle size as necessary to obtain correct gauge.

Pattern Notes

On the RS, all knit stitches are twisted (knit through the back loop), except the edge sts; on the WS, all purl stitches are twisted (purled through the back loop), except the edge sts. For simplicity in reading, twisted stitches are written as plain knit or purl.

Increases are all lifted increases and are worked on WS rows. Work as a lifted-increase left (LI-L) at the beginning of the row and as a lifted-increase right (LI-R) at the end of the row.

Special Abbreviations

LI-L (lifted increase-left): Insert tip of LH needle into left side of st 2 rows below st on RH needle and knit into it.

LI-R (lifted increase-right): Insert tip of RH needle into right side of st below st on LH needle and knit into it.

1/1 LC: Sl 1 to cn and hold in front; k1-tbl, k1-tbl from cn.

1/1 RC: Sl 1 to cn and hold in back; k1-tbl, k1-tbl from cn.

1/1 LPT: Sl 1 to cn and hold in front; p1-tbl, k1-tbl from cn.

1/1 RPT: Sl 1 to cn and hold in back; k1-tbl, p1-tbl from cn.

Stitch Patterns

Pattern A *(6 sts, inc to 20 sts)*

Row 1 (WS): P1 (edge st), k1, p2, k1, p1 (edge st).

Row 2 (RS): K1 (edge st), p1, 1/1 LC, p1, k1 (edge st).

Row 3: P1, k1, LI-L, p2, LI-R, k1, p1—8 sts.

Row 4: K1, p1, 1/1 RPT, 1/1 LPT, p1, k1.

Row 5: P1, k1, LI-L, p2, k2, p2, LI-R, k1, p1—10 sts.

Row 6: K1, p1, 1/1 RC, p2, 1/1 RC, p1, k1.

Row 7: P1, k1, LI-L, p2, k2, p2, LI-R, k1, p1—12 sts.

Row 8: K1, p1, [1/1 RPT, 1/1 LPT] twice, p1, k1.

Row 9: P1, k1, LI-L, p1, k2, p2, k2, p1, LI-R, k1, p1—14 sts.

Row 10: K1, p1, [1/1 LC, p2] twice, 1/1 LC, p1, k1.

Row 11: P1, k1, LI-L, [p2, k2] twice, p2, LI-R, k1, p1—16 sts.

Row 12: K1, p1, [1/1 RPT, 1/1 LPT] 3 times, p1, k1.

Row 13: P1, k1, LI-L, p1, [k2, p2] twice, k2, p1, LI-R, k1, p1—18 sts.

Row 14: K1, p1, [1/1 RC, p2] 3 times, 1/1 RC, p1, k1.

Row 15: P1, k1, LI-L, [p2, k2] 3 times, p2, LI-R, k1, p1—20 sts.

Row 16: K1, p1, [1/1 RPT, 1/1 LPT] 4 times, p1, k1.

Row 17: P1, k1, p1, [k2, p2] 3 times, k2, p1, k1, p1.

Pattern B *(20 sts, dec to 18 sts, inc to 26 sts)*

Row 1 (RS): K1, p1, k1, [p2, k2] 3 times, p2, k1, p1, k1.

Row 2: P1, k1, p1, [k2, p2] 3 times, k2, p1, k1, p1.

Row 3: K1, p1, [1/1 LPT, 1/1 RPT] 4 times, p1, k1.

Row 4: P1, ssk, [p2, k2] 3 times, p2, k2tog, p1—18 sts.

Row 5: K1, p1, [1/1 RC, p2] 3 times, 1/1 RC, p1, k1.

Row 6: P1, k1, LI-L, [p2, k2] 3 times, p2, LI-R, k1, p1—20 sts.

Row 7: K1, p1, [1/1 RPT, 1/1 LPT] 4 times, p1, k1.

Row 8: P1, k1, LI-L, p1, [k2, p2] 3 times, k2, p1, LI-R, k1, p1—22 sts.

Row 9: K1, p1, 1/1 RPT, [p2, 1/1 LC] 3 times, p2, 1/1 LPT, p1, k1.

Row 10: P1, k1, LI-L, p1, k3, [p2, k2] twice, p2, k3, p1, LI-R, k1, p1—24 sts.

Row 11: K1, p1, 1/1 RPT, p2, [1/1 RPT, 1/1 LPT] 3 times, p2, 1/1 LPT, p1, k1.

Row 12: P1, k1, LI-L, p1, k3, p1 [k2, p2] twice, k2, p1, k3, p1, LI-R, k1, p1—26 sts.

Row 13: K1, p1, [1/1 RPT, p2] twice, [1/1 RC, p2] twice, 1/1 LPT, p2, 1/1 LPT, p1, k1.

Row 14: P1, k1, [p1, k3] twice, p2, k2, p2, [k3, p1] twice, k1, p1.

Row 15: K1, p1, k1, [p2, 1/1 RPT] twice, 1/1 LPT, 1/1 RPT, [1/1/LPT, p2] twice, k1, p1, k1.

Row 16: P1, k1, p1, k2, p1, k3, p1, k2, p2, k2, p1, k3, p1, k2, p1, k1, p1.

Row 17: K1, p1, [k1, p2] twice, 1/1 RPT, p2, 1/1 LC, p2, 1/1 LPT, [p2, k1] twice, p1, k1.

Row 18: P1, k1, [p1, k2] twice, p1, k3, p2, k3, [p1, k2] twice, p1, k1, p1.

Row 19: K1, p1, [k1, p2] 3 times, 1/1 RPT, 1/1 LPT, [p2, k1] 3 times, p1, k1.

Row 20: P1, k1, [p1, k2] 7 times, p1, k1, p1.

Row 21: K1, p1, [k1, p2] 7 times, k1, p1, k1.

Row 22: Rep Row 20.

Row 23: Rep Row 21.

Row 24: Rep Row 20.

Row 25: K1, p1, [k1, p2] 3 times, 1/1 LPT, 1/1 RPT, [p2, k1] 3 times, p1, k1.

Row 26: P1, k1, [p1, k2] twice, p1, k3, p2, k3, [p1, k2] twice, p1, k1, p1.

Row 27: K1, p1, [k1, p2] twice, 1/1 LPT, p2, 1/1 LC, p2, 1/1 RPT, [p2, k1] twice, p1, k1.

Row 28: P1, k1, p1, k2, p1, k3, p1, k2, p2, k2, p1, k3, p1, k2, p1, k1, p1.

Row 29: K1, p1, k1, [p2, 1/1 LPT] twice, 1/1 RPT, 1/1 LPT, [1/1/RPT, p2] twice, k1, p1, k1.

Row 30: P1, k1, [p1, k3] twice, p2, k2, p2, [k3, p1] twice, k1, p1.

Row 31: K1, p1, [1/1 LPT, p2] twice, [1/1 RC, p2] twice, 1/1 RPT, p2, 1/1 RPT, p1, k1.

Row 32: P1, ssk, p1, k3, p1 [k2, p2] twice, k2, p1, k3, p1, k2tog, p1—24 sts.

Row 33: K1, p1, 1/1 LPT, p2, [1/1 LPT, 1/1 RPT] 3 times, p2, 1/1 RPT, p1, k1.

Row 34: P1, ssk, p1, k3, [p2, k2] twice, p2, k3, p1, k2tog, p1—22 sts.

Row 35: K1, p1, 1/1 LPT, [p2, 1/1 LC] 3 times, p2, 1/1 RPT, p1, k1.

Row 36: P1, ssk, p1, [k2, p2] 3 times, k2, p1, k2tog, p1—20 sts.

Row 37: K1, p1, [1/1 LPT,1/1 RPT] 4 times, p1, k1.

Row 38: P1, ssk, [p2, k2] 3 times, p2, k2tog, p1—18 sts.

Row 39: K1, p1, [1/1 RC, p2] 3 times, 1/1 RC, p1, k1.

Row 40: P1, k1, LI-L, [p2, k2] 3 times, p2, LI-R, k1, p1—20 sts.

Row 41: K1, p1, [1/1 RPT,1/1 LPT] 4 times, p1, k1.

Row 42: P1, k1, p1, [k2, p2] 3 times, k2, p1, k1, p1.

Pattern C (20 sts, dec to 6 sts)

Row 1 (RS): K1, p1, k1, p2, [1/1 LC, p2] 3 times, k1, p1, k1.

Row 2: P1, k1, p1, [k2, p2] 3 times, k2, p1, k1, p1.

Row 3: K1, p1, [1/1 LPT, 1/1 RPT] 4 times, p1, k1.

Row 4: P1, ssk, [p2, k2] 3 times, p2, k2tog, p1—18 sts.

Row 5: K1, p1, [1/1 RC, p2] 3 times, 1/1 RC, p1, k1.

Row 6: P1, ssk, p1, [k2, p2] twice, k2, p1, k2tog, p1—16 sts.

Row 7: K1, p1, [1/1 LPT, 1/1 RPT] 3 times, p1, k1.

Row 8: P1, ssk, [p2, k2] twice, p2, k2tog, p1—14 sts.

Row 9: K1, p1, [1/1 LC, p2] twice, 1/1 LC, p1, k1.

Row 10: P1, ssk, p1, k2, p2, k2, p1, k2tog, p1—12 sts.

Row 11: K1, p1, [1/1 LPT, 1/1 RPT] twice, p1, k1.

Row 12: P1, ssk, p2, k2, p2, k2tog, p1—10 sts.

Row 13: K1, p1, 1/1 RC, p2, 1/1 RC, p1, k1.

Row 14: P1, ssk, p1, k2, p1, k2tog, p1—8 sts.

Row 15: K1, p1, 1/1 LPT, 1/1 RPT, p1, k1.

Row 16: P1, ssk, p2, k2tog, p1—6 sts.

Row 17: K1, p1, 1/1 LC, p1, k1.

Row 18: P1, k1, p2, k1, p1.

Instructions

CO 6 sts.

Following Chart A or text instructions, work Pat A.

Following Chart B or text instructions, work Pat B 8 times or until scarf is 3" [7.6cm] short of the desired length (excluding tassels).

Following Chart C or text instructions, work Pat C.

BO in pat.

Finishing

Weave in all ends.

Block the scarf as desired.

Tassels

(Make 2)

Wind the yarn 40 times around an object (e.g., book, piece of cardboard) approx 4" [10cm] long. Cut yarn.

Cut a 12" [30.5cm] length of yarn and fold it in half; thread it through the tapestry needle.

Holding the yarn, push the tapestry needle under the center of the wound yarn loops at one end. Tie 2 double overhand knots. Pull the yarn snug.

Pull the tassel off the object and cut through the center of the opposite end of the yarn loops. Trim the ends evenly.

Secure a tassel to each end of the scarf.

STITCH KEY

- ☐ K1-tbl on RS, p1-tbl on WS
- ⊟ P1-tbl on RS, k1-tbl on WS
- ℝ LI-R
- 𝕃 LI-L
- K2tog on WS
- Ssk on WS
- 1/1 RC
- 1/1 LC
- 1/1 RPT
- 1/1 LPT

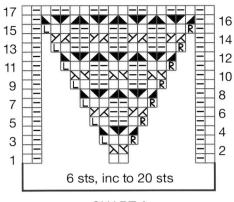

6 sts, inc to 20 sts

CHART A

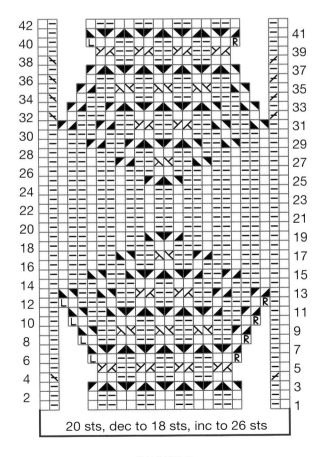

20 sts, dec to 18 sts, inc to 26 sts

CHART B

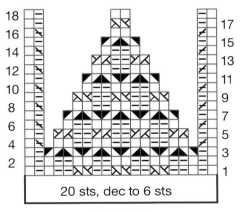

20 sts, dec to 6 sts

CHART C

European Cowl

Design by Donna Druchunas

As soon as the air begins to cool at the end of summer, scarves become a necessary part of the wardrobe in the Baltics—you are not properly dressed if you leave home without one. This versatile design is both fashionable and warm, and perfectly suited for the long, dark winters in the north. The scarf is inspired by my friend, Anna, a prolific and talented Estonian designer. The charted pattern is an adaptation of a traditional Estonian lace motif.

Finished Measurements
Circumference: 50" [127cm]

Width: 24" [61cm]

Materials 🧶4🧶
Plymouth *Baby Alpaca Worsted* (worsted weight; 100% baby alpaca; 102yds [93m] per 1¾ oz [50g] skein): 10 skeins Gray #402

Size 8 [5mm] circular needle or size needed to obtain gauge

Size H/8 [5mm] crochet hook (optional for provisional CO)

Spare needle

Tapestry needle

Gauge
20 sts and 22 rows = 4" [10cm] in Lace pat.

Adjust needle size as necessary to obtain correct gauge.

Special Abbreviation
Inc8: Turn 1 st into 9 sts as follows: ([k1, yo] 4 times, k1) all in 1 st.

Pattern Notes
This cowl is worked flat, then the cast-on stitches and last-row stitches are joined using 3-needle bind-off.

A circular needle accommodates the large number of stitches; do not join.

Special Techniques
Provisional Cast-On: With a crochet hook and waste yarn, make a chain several sts longer than the desired cast-on. With a knitting needle and project yarn, pick up indicated number of sts in the "bumps" on the back of the chain. When indicated in the pattern, "unzip" the crochet chain to free the live sts.

3-Needle Bind-Off: With RS together and needles parallel, using a 3rd needle, knit 1 st from the front needle together with 1 from the back. *Knit together 1 st from the front and back needles, then slip the first st over the 2nd to bind off. Rep from * across, then fasten off the last st.

Pattern Stitch

Lace Pattern (multiple of 14 sts [inc to 20 sts] + 2)

Note: Count sts only on Rows 1–2, 9–12, 19–20.

Row 1 (RS): P2, *k1, p2, k9, p2; rep from * to end—14 sts each rep.

Row 2 and all WS rows: Work all sts as they present themselves (knit the knits and purl the purls).

Row 3: P2, *inc8, p2, k3, sk2p, k3, p2; rep from * to end—20 sts each rep.

Row 5: P2, *k1, p7, k1, p2, k2, sk2p, k2, p2; rep from * to end—18 sts each rep.

Row 7: P2, *k9, p2, k1, sk2p, k1, p2; rep from * to end—16 sts each rep.

Row 9: P2, *k9, p2, sk2p, p2; rep from * to end—14 sts each rep.

Row 11: P2, *k9, p2, k1, p2; rep from * to end—14 sts each rep.

Row 13: P2, *k3, sk2p, k3, p2, inc8, p2; rep from * to end—20 sts each rep.

Row 15: P2, *k2, sk2p, k2, p2, k1, p7, k1, p2; rep from * to end—18 sts each rep.

Row 17: P2, *k1, sk2p, k1, p2, k9, p2; rep from * to end—16 sts each rep.

Row 19: P2, *sk2p, p2, k9, p2; rep from * to end—14 sts each rep.

Row 20: Work as for Row 2.

Rep Rows 1–20 for pat.

Instructions

Using your preferred method, provisionally CO 122 sts.

Row 1 (RS): K4, pm, work Row 1 of Lace pat, pm, k4.

Row 2 (and all WS rows): Knit the 4 edge sts at each side; work sts between markers as they present themselves (knit the knits and purl the purls).

Cont working Lace pat as est, working 20 rows for each rep, until piece measures approx 50" [127cm], ending with Row 1.

Finishing

Undo the provisional CO, placing live sts on a needle.

Join the ends to form a tube using 3-needle BO, being careful not to twist the fabric.

Wash the scarf and dry it flat to block. Do not flatten out the texture of the pattern stitch.

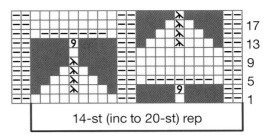

14-st (inc to 20-st) rep

LACE PATTERN

French "Coco"
Woven Scarf

Design by Elanor Lynn

Bring a little Parisian luxury chic to your wardrobe with this scarf, which is inspired by Coco Chanel and the Chanel-style suits that featured a woven plaid pattern. This clever design uses short rows to round the neck in a U shape, giving the scarf a very tailored and attractive look.

Finished Measurements

7" x 63" [18 x 160cm], excluding fringe

Materials [4]

Cascade Yarns *Dolce* (light worsted weight; 55% superfine alpaca/23% wool/22% silk; 109yds [100m] per 1¾ oz [50g] skein): 4 skeins Ivory #909 (A); 1 skein each Beige #940 (B) and Pink #960 (C)

Size 3 [3mm] needles

Size 5 [3.75mm] needles or size needed to obtain gauge

Size E/4 [3.5mm] crochet hook

Tapestry needle

Gauge

31 sts and 40 rows = 4" [10cm] in Woven Stripes pat on larger needles.

Adjust needle size as necessary to obtain correct gauge.

Pattern Notes

Each row is worked with 1 color of yarn. Change colors at the beginning of RS rows by twisting the working yarn around the nonworking yarns at the back.

The slipped stitches pull the color from the row below up to the current row. This effect is shown on the chart.

There is a 3-stitch garter stitch border at each edge.

The scarf is shaped like a U, creating a collar at the back neck; the shaping is worked using short rows.

For a simpler version, omit the shaping and work 63 pattern repeats.

Stitch Pattern

Woven Stripes Pattern (multiple of 9 sts + 4)

Row 1 (RS): With B, k1, *sl 2 wyib, k1, [sl 1 wyif, k1] 3 times; rep from * to last 3 sts, sl 2 wyib, k1.

Row 2: With B, p1, *sl 2 wyif, p7; rep from * to last 3 sts, sl 2 wyif, p1.

Row 3: With A, k3, *sl 1 wyif, [k1, sl 1 wyif] 3 times, k2; rep from * to last st, k1.

Row 4: With A, purl.

Rows 5 and 6: With C, rep Rows 1 and 2.

Rows 7 and 8: With A, rep Rows 3 and 4.

Row 9: With A, p1, *k2, p7; rep from * to last 3 sts, k2, p1.

Row 10: With A, k1, *p2, k7; rep from * to last 3 sts, p2, k1.

Rep Rows 1–10 for pat.

Instructions

First End

With smaller needles and A, CO 45 sts.

Knit 4 rows.

Change to larger needles and B; increase in pat as follows:

Row 1 (RS): K3 (edge sts), pm, k1, *sl 2 wyib, M1, sl 1 wyif, k1, sl 1 wyif, M1, sl 1 wyif, k1; rep from * to last 7 sts, sl 2 wyib, k1, pm, k3 (edge sts)—55 sts.

Maintaining first and last 3 sts in garter st and beg with Row 2 of the pat, work Woven Stripes pat between edge sts until 21 reps are complete.

Back Neck "Collar"

Cont in Woven Stripes pat, working short rows (no wraps) as follows:

Row 1 (RS): With B, k3, work pat over 19 sts, turn.

Row 2: [P7, sl 2 wyif] twice, p1, k3.

Row 3: With A, k3, work pat over 28 sts, turn.

Row 4: Purl to marker, k3.

Row 5: With C, k3, work pat over 37 sts, turn.

Row 6: [P7, sl 2 wyif] 4 times, p1, k3.

Row 7: With A, k3, work pat over 46 sts, turn.

Row 8: Purl to marker, k3.

Row 9: K3, work pat over 46 sts, turn.

Row 10: Purl to marker, k3.

Rows 11–20: Work est pat over all sts.

Rep [Rows 1–20] 10 more times.

Second End

Work 20 pat reps, ending with Row 9 on last rep.

Change to smaller needles.

Dec row (WS): K4, [k2, k2tog, k3, ssk] 5 times, k6—45 sts.

Knit 3 rows.

BO with larger needles.

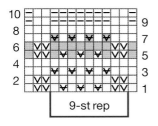

STITCH AND COLOR KEY

☐ With A, k on RS, p on WS
☐ With B, k on RS, p on WS
▨ With C, k on RS, p on WS
☑ Sl 1 wyib
☒ Sl 1 wyif
⊟ With A, p on RS, k on WS

WOVEN STRIPES

Finishing

Weave in the ends. Block the scarf.

Fringe

Cut 96 strands of MC 11" [28cm] long. Attach
24 fringes evenly spaced along one short end as
follows: With 2 strands held tog and folded in half,
use a crochet hook to pull the folded loop from
the RS to the WS; pull the ends through the loop
and tighten. Repeat on the other short end. Trim
the fringe to the desired length.

Celtic Felted-Flower Scarf

Design by Melissa Wehrle

This modern Aran scarf was inspired by the intricate Aran sweaters of the Aran Islands off the coast of Ireland. Traditionally these sweaters were knit out of unscoured cream-colored wool, which offered very good protection from wet weather conditions—a great benefit to the fishermen for whom the sweaters were knit. Cable patterns were usually unique to the county, parish, or township where the wearer lived, and sometimes the owner's initials were also knit into the design. To add a modern twist, I chose a natural heather gray wool that shows off the cable work beautifully. This pattern gets a floral touch with a few felted flowers trimmed with accents of contrasting-colored embroidery. Don't be afraid of the felting or embroidery! Any novice can handle the finishing work with ease.

Finished Measurements

7" x 82" [18 x 208cm], excluding fringe

Materials ▨4▨

Brown Sheep *Lanaloft Worsted* (worsted weight; 100% wool; 160yds [146m] per 3½ oz [100g] skein): 4 skeins Manor Grey #LL33W (MC) and 1 skein Buoyant Blue #LL47 (CC)

Size 8 [5mm] needles or size needed to obtain gauge

Size 9 [5.5mm] needles or size needed to obtain gauge

Size H/8 [5mm] crochet hook for attaching fringe

Sharp embroidery needle

Gauge

24 sts and 44 rows = 4" [10cm] over Cable Panel pat with larger needles.

17 sts and 22 rows = 4" [10cm] in St st with smaller needles (unfelted).

19 sts and 31 rows = 4" [10cm] St st with smaller needles (felted).

Adjust needle size as necessary to obtain correct gauge.

Special Abbreviations

1/1 LC: Sl 1 to cn and hold in front; k1, k1 from cn.

1/1 RC: Sl 1 to cn and hold in back; k1, k1 from cn.

2/1 LPC: Sl 2 to cn and hold in front; p1, k2 from cn.

2/1 RPC: Sl 1 to cn and hold in back; k2, p1 from cn.

2/2 LC: Sl 2 to cn and hold in front; k2, k2 from cn.

2/2 RC: Sl 2 to cn and hold in back; k2, k2 from cn.

2/1/2 LPC: Sl 3 to cn and hold in front; k2, slip purl st from cn to LH needle and p1, k2 from cn.

2/1/2 RPC: Sl 3 to cn and hold in back; k2, slip purl st from cn to LH needle and p1, k2 from cn.

Stitch Pattern

Cable Panel (41-st panel)

Row 1 (WS): K1, p1, k2, p2, k2, p4, [k2, p2] twice, k1, [p2, k2] twice, p4, k2, p2, k2, p1, k1.

Row 2 (RS): [K1, p1] twice, 1/1 RC, p2, 1/1 LC, 1/1 RC, p2, k2, p2, 2/1/2 RPC, p2, k2, p2, 1/1 LC, 1/1 RC, p2, 1/1 RC, [p1, k1] twice.

Row 3: Rep Row 1.

Row 4: [K1, p1] twice, 1/1 RC, p2, 1/1 RC, 1/1 LC, p2, 2/1 LPC, 2/1 RPC, p1, 2/1 LPC, 2/1 RPC, p2, 1/1 RC, 1/1 LC, p2, 1/1 RC, [p1, k1] twice.

Row 5: K1, p1, k2, p2, k2, p4, [k3, p4] 3 times, k2, p2, k2, p1, k1.

Row 6: [K1, p1] twice, 1/1 RC, p2, 1/1 LC, 1/1 RC, p3, 2/2 RC, p3, 2/2 LC, p3, 1/1 LC, 1/1 RC, p2, 1/1 RC, [p1, k1] twice.

Row 7: Rep Row 5.

Row 8: [K1, p1] twice, 1/1 RC, p2, 1/1 RC, 1/1 LC, p2, 2/1 RPC, 2/1 LPC, p3, 2/1 RPC, 2/1 LPC, p2, 1/1 RC, 1/1 LC, p2, 1/1 RC, [p1, k1] twice.

Row 9: Rep Row 1.

Row 10: [K1, p1] twice, 1/1 RC, p2, 1/1 LC, 1/1 RC, p2, k2, p2, 2/1/2 LPC, p2, k2, p2, 1/1 LC, 1/1 RC, p2, 1/1 RC, [p1, k1] twice.

Rows 11–16: Rep Rows 3–8.

Rep Rows 1–16 for pat.

Instructions

With larger needles, CO 41 sts.

Work 2 rows of K1, P1 Rib.

Rep 16-row Cable Panel pat until scarf measures 82" [208.5cm] or desired length, ending with Row 16.

Work 2 rows of K1, P1 Rib.

BO in rib.

Finishing

Felted Flowers

With smaller needles, CO 41 sts.

Work in St st until the piece measures 9½" [24cm].

Felt the piece in a washing machine and allow it to dry.

Using flower templates as a guide, cut out 1 piece each from felt; cut out centers.

Embroidery

Cut a length of CC.

Work blanket stitch around the center of each flower.

Work running stitch on each petal.

With tapestry needle and MC, sew flowers onto one end of scarf, positioning each flower as desired.

Fringe

Cut 54 strands of MC 10" [25.5cm] long. Attach 9 fringes evenly spaced along each short end as follows: With 3 strands held together and folded in half, use a crochet hook to pull the folded loop from the RS to the WS; pull the ends through the loop and tighten. Trim the fringe to the desired length.

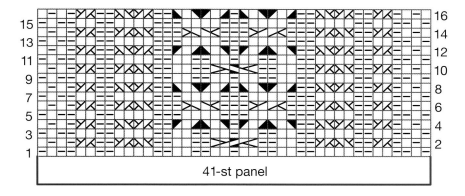

CABLE PANEL

STITCH KEY

☐ K on RS, p on WS
⊟ P on RS, k on WS
⬚ 1/1 RC
⬚ 1/1 LC
⬛ 2/1 RPC
⬛ 2/1 LPC
⬚ 2/2 RC
⬚ 2/2 LC
⬚ 2/1/2 RPC
⬚ 2/1/2 LPC

FLOWER TEMPLATES
Enlarge by 78%

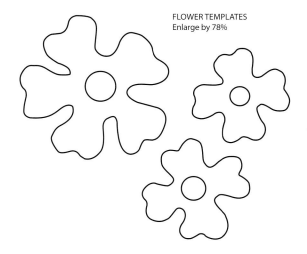

Stranded
Fair Isle Scarf

Design by Melissa Leapman

Here's a scarf inspired by the sweater motifs popular on Fair Isle, one of the Shetland Islands located north of Scotland. In keeping with the Fair Isle knitting tradition, the two colors in this scarf are not repeated for more than three consecutive stitches. This scarf is worked in the round, so there are no purl rows and no unsightly strands on the "wrong" side.

Finished Measurements
7" x 36" [18 x 91.5cm]

Materials 🧶2
Cascade Yarn *220 Sport* (sport weight; 100% wool; 164yds [150m] per 1¾ oz [50g] ball): 2 balls each Spring Green #8910 (A) and Azure Teal #8892 (B)

Size 5 [3.75mm] 16" [40cm] circular needle or size needed to obtain gauge

Stitch markers

Gauge
22 sts and 24 rnds = 4" [10cm] in stranded 2-color St st.

Adjust needle size as necessary to obtain correct gauge.

Pattern Note
There are two 1-stitch "edge stitches" between the two repeats. On one rnd, these stitches will be slipped purlwise with the yarn in back; on alternate rnds, these stitches will be knitted with B. The scarf will fold naturally at these edge stitches.

Stitch Pattern

Colorwork Pattern (multiple of 10 sts)

See Color Chart at right.

Instructions

With B, [CO 41 sts, pm] twice, placing 2nd marker for beg of rnd. Join, being careful not to twist sts.

Rnd 1: [Sl 1 wyib (edge st), work Rnd 1 of chart over next 40 sts] twice.

Rnd 2: [K1 B (edge st), work Rnd 2 of chart over next 40 sts] twice.

Cont in this manner, working Rnds 1–10 of chart and alternating slipping and knitting the edge sts, until the piece measures approx 36" [91.5cm], ending with Rnd 10 of chart.

BO with B.

Finishing

Keeping edge sts at the sides of the scarf, neatly sew the cast-on and bound-off edges together, closing each end of the scarf.

Wet-block to set sts.

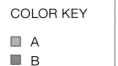

COLOR KEY

■ A
■ B

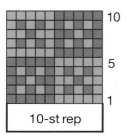

10-st rep

COLOR CHART

Cabled
Aran-Inspired Scarf

Design by Teva Durham

This romantic scarf is not only stylish and quick-to-knit, but also a fun exploration of the potential of cable patterns to morph the contours of a piece. This scarf riffs on the traditional Aran XOX pattern. The cabled "kisses and hugs" feature an extra braid to each X and reverse directions. In addition, the cabled pattern travels outward at each end of the scarf, providing jaunty flounces. A brioche rib offers a sturdy but airy background that will stay flat. Brioche is a fun and useful technique accomplished by slipping the column of knit stitches while working a yarn over that provides textural, wafflelike ladders that create a bridge at each side of a purled column.

Finished Measurements
Length: 42" [106.5cm]

Width: 11" [28cm] at ends, 5½" [14cm] in center

Materials 🧶4️⃣
Loop-d-Loop by Teva Durham
New Birch (worsted weight; 65% cotton/35% silk; 98yds [89.5m] per 1¾ oz [50g] ball): 4 balls Maize #13

Size 6 [4mm] needles

Cable needle

Tapestry needle

Gauge
16 sts and 20 rows = 4" [10cm] over Brioche Rib (unstretched).

Adjust needle size as necessary to obtain correct gauge.

Pattern Note
The background of this scarf is a Brioche Rib. When working Brioche Rib, slip stitches pwise. The first several rows of the pattern are written out to get you started, after which you will just follow the charts to the end.

Special Technique
Brioche Rib: After the initial set-up row, all rows are worked in same way: 2 stitches alternate as for regular rib, with one stitch being worked as a slipped stitch with a yo and the other stitch purling together the yo and slipped stitch of the previous row. Once you get accustomed to working Brioche Rib, it becomes second nature.

Pattern Stitches

See charts.

Instructions

First End

CO 55 sts.

Row 1 (Set-up, WS): K1, p1, [sl 1/yo, p1] twice, k1; p4; k1, p1, sl 1/yo, p1, k1; p4; k1, p1, [sl 1/yo, p1] 6 times, k1; p4; k1, p1, sl 1/yo, p1, k1; p4; k1, p1, [sl 1/yo, p1] twice, k1.

Row 2 (RS): K1, sl 1/yo, [p2tog (the sl 1/yo of previous row), sl 1/yo] twice, p1; k4; p1, sl 1/yo, p2tog, sl 1/yo, p1; k4; p1, sl 1/yo, [p2tog, sl 1/yo] 6 times, p1; k4; p1, sl 1/yo, p2tog, sl 1/yo, p1; k4; p1, sl 1/yo, [p2tog, sl 1/yo] twice, k1.

Row 3: K1, p2tog, [sl 1/yo, p2tog] twice, k1; p4; k1, p2tog, sl 1/yo, p2tog, k1; p4; k1, p2tog, [sl 1/yo, p2tog] 6 times, k1; p4; k1, p2tog, sl 1/yo, p2tog, k1; p4; k1, p2tog, [sl 1/yo, p2tog] twice, k1.

Rows 4 and 5: Rep Rows 2 and 3.

Row 6: K1, sl 1/yo, [p2tog, sl 1/yo] twice, p1; k3, ssk; sl 1/yo, p2tog, sl 1/yo, p1; k4; p1, sl 1/yo, [p2tog, sl 1/yo] 6 times, p1; k4; p1, sl 1/yo, p2tog, sl 1/yo; k2tog, k3; p1, sl 1/yo, [p2tog, sl 1/yo] twice, k1—53 sts.

Row 7: K1, p2tog, [sl 1/yo, p2tog] twice, k1; p4; p2tog, sl 1/yo, p2tog, k1; p4; k1, p2tog, [sl 1/yo, p2tog] 6 times, k1; p4; k1, p2tog, sl 1/yo, p2tog; p4; k1, p2tog, [sl 1/yo, p2tog] twice, k1.

Rows 8-33: Cont working Chart 1 for the bottom of the scarf—39 sts at end of Chart 1.

Central Section

Work [Chart 2] 6 times or until scarf measures approx 4" [10cm] short of desired length.

Second End

Work Chart 3—55 sts at end of Chart 3.

BO very loosely in pat.

Finishing

Weave in ends and block the scarf as desired.

STITCH KEY

- ☐ K on RS, p on WS
- ⊟ P on RS, k on WS
- ✳ P2tog on RS, sl1/yo on WS
- ⌒ Sl1/yo on RS, p2tog on WS
- ◩ K2tog
- ◺ Ssk
- ◪ P3tog
- Ⓜ M1 kwise on RS
- Ⓜ M1 pwise on RS, m1 kwise on WS
- ◼ No stitch
- ⊏▷◺⊤⊦◺⊏ Sl 4 to cn and hold in back, K4, k4 from cn
- ⊏▷◺⊤⊦◺⊏ Sl 4 to cn and hold in front, k4, k4 from cn

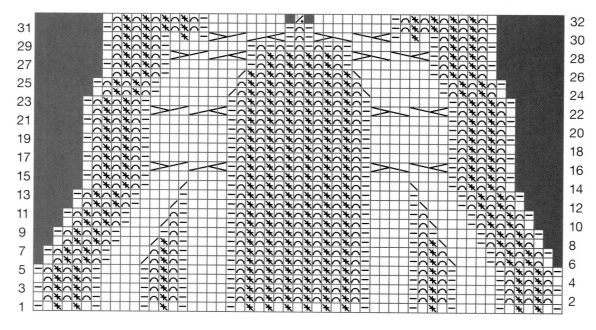

CHART 1 (FIRST END)

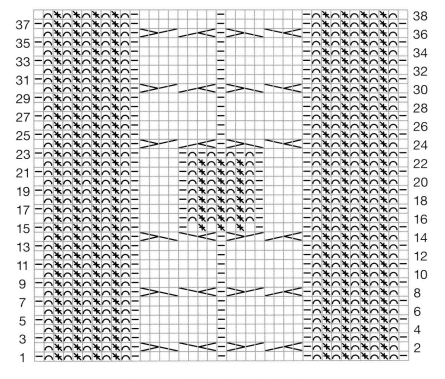

CHART 2 (CENTRAL SECTION)

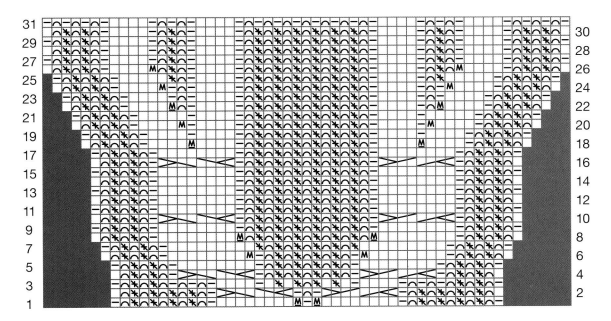

CHART 3 (SECOND END)

Chinese Good Fortune Scarf

Design by Lily M. Chin

While knitting is not historically an Asian tradition, it is widespread and popular throughout China and Japan. The double happiness symbol is used primarily during weddings in Chinese culture. Using the double-knit technique for a scarf makes sense for total reversibility. This two-color design results in a positive-negative configuration. One side has red symbols on a gold background; the other has gold symbols on a red background. The technique is simple yet intriguing.

Finished Measurements
5½" x 72" [14 x 183cm] or desired length

Materials ▧**1**▧
Bijou Basin *Bijou Spun* (fingering weight; 100% yak down; 100yds [91.5m] per 1oz [28g] skein): 3 skeins each Ruby (A) and Goldenrod (B)

Size 4 [3.5mm] needles

Size E/4 [3.5mm] crochet hook

Smooth waste yarn of similar weight in a contrasting color

Tapestry needle

Gauge
24 sts and 31 rows = 4" [10cm] on one side of double-knit fabric.

Adjust needle size as necessary to obtain correct gauge.

Pattern Notes
This scarf is worked using the double-knit technique. Both colors are used across all of the rows in pairs.

Twist the colors of yarn at the beginning of the rows to prevent holes.

The first several rows of double knitting are written out; the rest are charted and worked in the same manner.

There are 3 charts: Chart A shows one side of the double-knit pattern on one end of the scarf as it will look knitted up; the other side of the fabric will have the colors reversed and the other end of the scarf will have the same symbols upside down. Charts B and C are constructed so that you can work each side of the fabric more intuitively. Odd-numbered rows are worked with red (A) being the dominant background color, and even-numbered rows are worked with yellow (B) being the dominant background color. Turn your work when you get to the center of the chart. Rows can be read from left to right or right to left because the symbols are mirrored.

Instructions

First End

With B and using the Double-Knit Cast-On method, CO 67 sts into 34 crochet chains.

Row 1: With A, k2tog, *bring both yarns to front, p1 B, bring both yarns to back, k1 A; rep from * to last st, bring both yarns to front, p1 B—66 sts (33 sts per side).

Note: Remember to twist colors at beg of every row to prevent holes.

Row 2: *K1 B, bring both yarns to front, p1 A, bring both yarns to back; rep from * across.

Row 3: *K1 A, bring both yarns to front, p1 B, bring both yarns to back; rep from * across.

Row 4: [K1 B, bring both yarns to front, p1 A, bring both yarns to back] 5 times, *[k1 A, bring both yarns to front, p1 B, bring both yarns to back] twice, [k1 B, bring both yarns to front, p1 A, bring both yarns to back] 4 times, [k1 A, bring both yarns to front, p1 B, bring both yarns to back] twice**, [k1 B, bring both yarns to front, p1

A, bring both yarns to back] 6 times; rep from * to **, [k1 B, bring both yarns to front, p1 A, bring both yarns to back] 5 times.

Row 5: [K1 A, bring both yarns to front, p1 B, bring both yarns to back] 5 times, *[k1 B, bring both yarns to front, p1 A, bring both yarns to back] twice, [k1 A, bring both yarns to front, p1 B, bring both yarns to back] 4 times, [k1 B, bring both yarns to front, p1 A, bring both yarns to back] twice **, [k1 A, bring both yarns to front, p1 B, bring both yarns to back] 6 times; rep from * to **, [k1 A, bring both yarns to front, p1 B, bring both yarns to back] 5 times.

Cont to work Chart B until Row 55 has been completed.

Center Section

Row 56: *[K1 B, bring both yarns to front, p1 A, bring both yarns to back] 3 times, [k1 A, bring both yarns to front, p1 B, bring both yarns to back] 3 times; rep from * 4 times more, end [k1 B, bring both yarns to front, p1 A, bring both yarns to back] 3 times.

Row 57: *[K1 A, bring both yarns to front, p1 B, bring both yarns to back] 3 times, [k1 B, bring both yarns to front, p1 A, bring both yarns to back] 3 times; rep from * 4 times more, end [k1 A, bring both yarns to front, p1 B, bring both yarns to back] 3 times.

Row 58: As for Row 56.

Rep Rows 57 and 58 until the scarf measures 65" [165cm] or 7" [18cm] short of desired length.

2nd End

Follow Chart C to the end.

Finishing

With either A or B, graft ends of scarf together using Kitchener st; if desired, transfer each side's sts to separate needles before grafting. Pull out the cast-on waste yarn. Block the scarf. Weave the ends into the hollow inside.

STITCH AND COLOR KEY

■ With both yarns in back, k1 with Red (A); with both yarns in front, p1 with Yellow (B)

□ With both yarns in back, k1 with Yellow (B); with both yarns in front, p1 with Red (A)

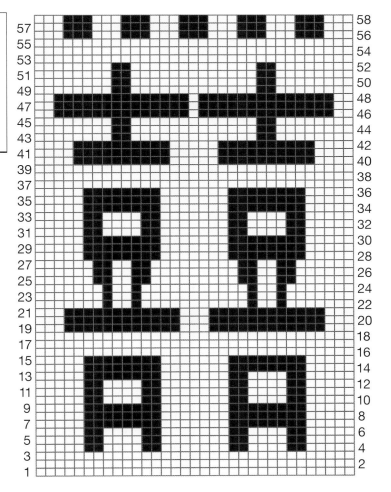

CHART A: BOTTOM OF YELLOW DOMINANT SIDE

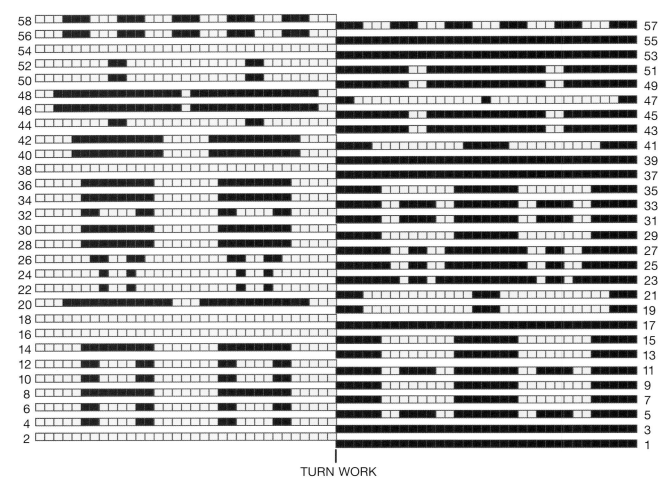

TURN WORK

33 SETS OF STS: YELLOW DOMINANT SIDE   33 SETS OF STS: RED DOMINANT SIDE

CHART B

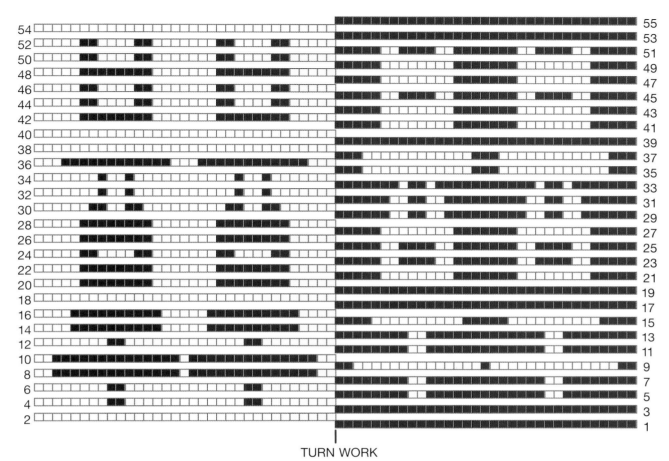

TURN WORK

33 SETS OF STS: YELLOW DOMINANT SIDE   33 SETS OF STS: RED DOMINANT SIDE

CHART C

Pendleton Scarf

Design by Lucy Neatby

This design came about by a circuitous route. Whilst visiting Tacoma, Washington, I was bewitched by the beautiful glass designs that can be found all over the city. Tacoma is also the birthplace of the world-renowned glass sculptor Dale Chihuly. Whilst reading about his work, I came across his series of glass works inspired by his collection of Native American trade blankets, which caused me to take another look at these blankets and their gorgeous, bold designs. Oregon-based Pendleton Woolen Mills, one of the major producers of these blankets, has used this style of weaving since the early twentieth century.

Although I've always been drawn to this style of motif, it doesn't lend itself well to interpretation in stranded (or two-color-per-row) knitting, where long floats of unused colors present difficulties. Double-layer knitting, on the other hand, is the perfect way to interpret them; both colors are used at all times to produce a reversible fabric reminiscent of the original blankets.

Finished Measurements

6¼" x 48" [16 x 122cm] or desired length

Materials 🧶4

Noro *Kureyon* (worsted weight; 100% wool; 109yds [100m] per 1¾ oz [50g] ball): 2 balls variegated Green, Teal, Purple, Red #220 (A)*

Brown Sheep *Lamb's Pride Worsted* (worsted weight; 85% wool/15% mohair; 190yds [174m] per 4oz [113g] skein): 1 skein Deep Charcoal #M06 (B)*

Size 10 [6mm] needles

Size 8 [5mm] needle (optional for tubular cast-on)

Tapestry needle

Note: For the sake of your sanity, choose strongly contrasting light and dark yarns for your first scarf!

Gauge

13½ sts and 17 rows = 4" [10cm] on one side of double-knit fabric.

Aim for a soft fabric with a pleasing scarflike drape. In order to achieve a soft fabric you will probably require needles slightly larger than usual for regular St st in your yarn.

Special Abbreviations

Side X: This is the side of the scarf depicted by the chart; odd-numbered rows are worked with the X side facing.

Side Y: This is the reverse side of the scarf, which is not depicted by the chart: even-numbered rows are worked with the Y side facing.

Nearside Fabric: The layer of fabric nearest to the knitter; these stitches are always knitted.

Farside Fabric: The layer of fabric farthest from the knitter; these stitches are always purled.

Swing (sw): Swing both yarns between the needles (forward if next stitch is a purl stitch, back if next stitch is a knit stitch).

Pattern Notes

The scarf has two public sides and will therefore require twice as many stitches as charted.

The purpose of swinging the yarns back and forth between the needles after each stitch is to keep the nonworking yarn between the two layers of fabric. The action should feel similar to working a 1x1 rib.

Don't allow the 2 working yarns to twist around each other. Always keep the Near Yarn in front of the Far Yarn. The 2 fabrics will then only be connected at the side of a color change.

There is no private side on which to hide any ends; join the yarns by splicing when necessary.

The edge stitches of double-knitted fabric are always a little less than pristine. Don't let them trouble you!

Technical Notes

Casting On

Two options are offered. Try each on your practice swatch to see the different results.

Conventional Cast-On: With B, using Long-Tail Cast-On or your preferred method, cast on the required number of stitches (keep the stitches close together). If using this method, finish with the Condensed Bind-Off.

Tubular Cast-On: This is my favored method, but it is a bit tricky to get used to at first. Use a straight needle to cast on (even when you plan to work the remainder with a circular needle) because a straight needle prevents the stitches from deforming before you have a chance to work the first row. *(Use a needle 1 or 2 sizes smaller than your main working needle for the cast-on row to prevent the edge from flaring.)*

Set-up: Tie both yarns together near the ends with a slip knot. Place this slip knot on your needle (do not count this as a stitch). Hold the needle in your right hand with the 2 yarns spread apart in the left hand (have B nearest to you) and the needle tip pointing above the yarns. Keep a gentle tension on both yarns at all times. Place a finger of the right hand on the slip knot to keep it on the needle to begin.

Step 1: Swing the needle tip toward you, over B, down and back under B, away from you and over A, down under A and back toward you, passing under B also. Lift the needle tip back to the starting position. You should now have 1 stitch of A on the needle.

Step 2: Push the needle tip away from you, over A, down and back toward you underneath both A and B, lift the needle tip up and over B and away from you and back under A. Lift the needle tip into the starting position. You should now have 2 stitches on the needle, the newest one being in B and resembling a purl stitch.

Repeat these steps until you have the desired number of stitches. Ensure that the yarn forming the new stitch runs right around the needle. Since you are making an even number of stitches, the final stitch should be a B stitch.

Binding Off

Condensed Bind-Off: Cut A. With the single strand of B, work the first 3 sts in 1x1 Rib (i.e., k1, p1, k1), lift the first st worked over the other 2 stitches on the RH needle (similar to a regular bind-off), *work the next stitch in rib as appropriate, bind off the outermost RH stitch as before; repeat from * until 2 stitches remain. Cut the yarn and bring the tail through both stitches and neaten them using the tail.

Tubular Bind-Off (Grafted)

Set-up: Using the appropriate color, work 1 row on the farside (purl) stitches only: *Sl 1 wyib, p1; repeat from * to end. Cut this yarn only.

Slide the work back to the opposite end of the needle (or onto another needle if using straights) and cut the remaining nearside yarn, leaving a tail 4 times the width of the fabric.

The nearside stitches can now be grafted to the farside stitches: We will use a tapestry needle to insert a connecting row of stitches. *(This is much easier to do than to put into words!)*

If you are nervous, thread a safety line of fine yarn through all the stitches before you begin: Either thread all the stitches onto a single yarn, or put the nearside and farside stitches onto separate threads.

As the stitches are sewn into place, adjust the stitches to correspond in size with the regularly worked stitches.

Grafting Instructions for Double-Knit Fabric

Back and front refer to the sides of the fabric, the front being nearest to the knitter.

It is assumed that the first st on the needle is a knit st and that your sts are sitting on the needle conventionally (with the right leg in front of the needle).

1. Slip Stitch #1 (a nearside knit stitch) off the needle and to the front (hold it with your thumb or a pin if you wish).

2. With a tapestry needle threaded with the tail of yarn from St #1, enter Stitch #2 (a farside purl) as if to knit (front to back), draw through the yarn but do not stretch Stitch #1. Drop Stitch #2 from the needle. Replace Stitch #1 correctly on the needle.

3. With the tapestry needle, enter Stitch #1 as if to knit, draw the yarn through and allow this stitch to drop off the needle.

4. Enter Stitch #3 (a nearside knit) as if to purl, draw the yarn through. Drop Stitch #3 from the needle.

5. Enter Stitch #2 (the farside purl already dropped) from back to front (if you chose to replace this stitch on the needle, this would be as if to purl, then allow it to drop). Draw the yarn through.

6. Enter Stitch #4 as if to knit, allow it to drop off the needle. Draw the yarn through.

This routine can now be broken down into an easy, 2-step process. Stitches are now dropped as soon as the needle has threaded them. Adjust the size of the sewn stitches to correspond with the regular knitted stitches.

1. Re-enter Stitch #3 (a nearside knit currently off the needle) from front to back as if to knit, enter the next stitch on the needle (a nearside knit) as if to purl, drop this stitch from the needle and draw the yarn through.

2. Re-enter Stitch #4 (a farside purl currently off the needle) from back to front as if to purl, enter the next stitch on the needle (a farside purl) as if to knit, drop this stitch and draw the yarn through.

Repeat the last 2 steps. If you are looking for this process in a reference book, see the directions for Tubular Bind-Off for Single Rib.

Reading Charts

Each box on the chart represents a pair of stitches: A pair consists of a nearside knit and a farside purl st. Pairs of stitches are always worked in opposite colors.

Double-knit fabric has 2 public sides: Side X and Side Y. The chart is drawn showing Side X facing.

A blank square on a Side X row is a variegated (A) knit st followed by solid-colored (B) purl st.

A dark square on a Side X row is a solid-colored (B) knit st followed by variegated (A) purl st.

A blank square on a Side Y row is a solid-colored (B) knit st followed by variegated (A) purl st.

A dark square on a Side Y row is a variegated (A) knit st followed by solid-colored purl st.

Instructions

Important note: Before beginning each new row, ensure that the yarn attached to the 2nd stitch lies over the top of the yarn attached to the outermost stitch (it will then be trapped when the first stitch is worked); this will join the sides.

Using whichever method you choose, CO 42 sts.

Set-Up Row 1: *K1 B, swing both yarns between the needles (sw), p1 A, sw; rep from * to end. This will produce 1 row of St st on each side of the fabric. The colors should run continuously across the row on each side.

Set-Up Row 2: *K1 A, sw, p1 B, sw; rep from * to end.

One side of your scarf should be in B, the other in A.

For simplicity, Set-Up Rows 1 and 2 could be rewritten:

Set-Up Row 1: *KB/pA; rep from * to end.

Set-Up Row 2: *KA/pB; rep from * to end.

The remainder of the stitch instructions will be written in this manner.

Pattern (also shown on the chart)

Row 1: [KB/pA] 8 times, [kA/pB] 5 times, [kB/pA] 8 times.

Row 2: [KA/pB] 9 times, [kB/pA] 3 times, [kA/pB] 9 times.

Row 3: [KB/pA] 10 times, [kA/pB] once, [kB/pA] 10 times.

Row 4: [KA/pB] 5 times, [kB/pA] 5 times, [kA/pB] once, [kB/pA] 5 times, [kA/pB] 5 times.

Row 5: [KB/pA] 6 times, [kA/pB] 3 times, [kB/pA] 3 times, [kA/pB] 3 times, [kB/pA] 6 times.

Row 6: [KA/pB] 7 times, [kB/pA] once, [kA/pB] 5 times, [kB/pA] once, [kA/pB] 7 times.

Row 7: [KB/pA] twice, [kA/pB] 5 times, [kB/pA] 3 times, [kA/pB] once, [kB/pA] 3 times, [kA/pB] 5 times, [kB/pA] twice.

Row 8: [KA/pB] 3 times, [kB/pA] 3 times, [kA/pB] 4 times, [kB/pA] once, [kA/pB] 4 times, [kB/pA] 3 times, [kA/pB] 3 times.

Row 9: [KB/pA] 4 times, [kA/pB] once, [kB/pA] 3 times, [kA/pB] 5 times, [kB/pA] 3 times, [kA/pB] once, [kB/pA] 4 times.

Row 10: Rep Row 8.

Row 11: Rep Row 7.

Row 12: Rep Row 6.

Row 13: Rep Row 5.

Row 14: Rep Row 4.

Row 15: Rep Row 3.

Row 16: Rep Row 2.

Row 17: Rep Row 1.

Row 18: *KA/pB; rep from * to end.

Row 19: *KB/pA; rep from * to end.

Row 20: Rep Row 18.

Rep Rows 1–20 until scarf is desired length, ending with Row 20.

Rep Set-Up Rows 1 and 2, matching colors A and B to correspond with the cast-on edge.

BO using either the condensed or tubular method.

Finishing

If you have ends to hide: Untie the clumps of ends along the sides and re-pair them into groups of 2 (1 from each fabric). Tie these pairs into a permanent overhand knot. Put a needle into the middle of the knot and use the needle to slide the knot up to the edge of the fabric before tightening it firmly. (While the needle is in the middle of the knot, you are free to adjust the position of the knot as it cannot irreversibly clamp up.)

Clip yarn tails to 4" [10cm] and thread them as far as possible in between the two layers of the scarf. Before releasing the tails from the needle, give the tails a little tug to pull the knot between the layers.

Block the scarf as desired.

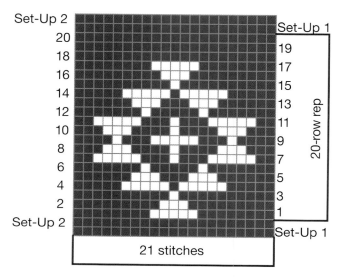

PENDLETON CHART SIDE X

Central Park
Möbius-Strip Scarf

Design by Jennifer Hansen

This luxurious scarf, knit in soft cashmere, is the perfect accessory for adding a little warmth and glamour to a late autumn walk through Central Park. The clever Möbius-strip design is essentially a tube of knitting with a twist, making it easy to wrap and wear in a number of ways. Once you master the Möbius strip Cast-On, popularized by Cat Bordhi, this project is a simple matter of knit and purl rounds: a great project for mindless, on-the-go knitting.

Finished Measurements
Circumference: 44" [112cm]

Width: 18" [45.5cm]

Materials 🧶3🧶
Stitch Diva Studios *Studio Cashmere* (DK weight; 100% cashmere; 165yds [150m] per 1¾ oz [50g] skein): 3 skeins #22 Ruby

Size 6 [4mm] circular needle, 47–60" [120–150cm] long or size needed to obtain gauge

Stitch marker

Tapestry needle

Gauge
14 sts and 27 rnds = 4" [10cm] in St st.

Adjust needle size as necessary to obtain correct gauge.

Pattern Note
If you have never knit a Möbius strip before, you are in for a treat. Knitting a Möbius strip calls for a long circular needle and a very special cast-on. This cast-on is double sided and is actually in the middle of the fabric once you have completed the strip. As you work, your knitting will grow between the overlapped cord of your long circular needle. There is only one bound-off edge, and every round you complete when knitting feels like two: Each round is comprised of two levels of stitches, one on either side of the cast-on round. You will work rounds of knit stitches and rounds of purl stitches following a Fibonacci sequence that you will see mirrored on either side of the cast-on. Finally, you will complete the project with a super stretchy bind-off. It is critical that the bind-off for this scarf be very stretchy. Keep in mind that the bind-off row itself will likely not be visible because of the rolled stockinette hem.

Special Techniques

Möbius Cast-On

Designer Cat Bordhi developed this ingenious multidirectional cast-on. This technique requires a very long circular needle as specified in the materials list.

Step 1: Make a slip knot and place it on the LH circular needle tip, then scoot the slip knot off the needle to the cable.

Step 2: Home Position—Hold the RH needle with the right hand, pinching the slip knot and left cable with the right thumb, keeping the working yarn behind the left cable. With the left hand, pinch the cable and keep the tension on the yarn.

Step 3: Scoop a Loop from Below—Bring the RH needle to the front of the cable, then under the cable to the back, coming up between the cable and the working yarn, then over the top of working yarn and behind it to scoop it back under the cable to the Home Position (Step 2).

Step 4: Scoop a Loop from Above—Bring the RH needle to the top of the cable, over the top of the yarn and then under the yarn to scoop up a loop, returning back to the Home Position.

Rep Steps 3 and 4, scooping up loops.

These instructions specify to CO 170, so you will scoop 169 times, with the slip knot counting as the first stitch.

Note: *For Cat Bordhi's video-tutorial for the Möbius Cast-On, go to http://www.youtube.com/watch?v=LVnTda7F2V4.*

Jeny's Super Stretchy Bind-Off

This bind-off is worked like a classic bind-off but with an additional yarnover before each stitch.

Step 1: Make a yarnover on the RH needle, bringing the yarn around the needle in the opposite direction than is customary.

Step 2: Knit the next stitch as usual.

Step 3: Insert the LH needle into the yarnover and pull it over the stitch that was just knit.

Step 4: Rep Steps 1–3, resulting in 2 stitches on the right needle. Pass the first st over the 2nd stitch.

Rep Step 4 until all stitches are bound off.

Note: *For a photo-tutorial for Jeny's Super Stretchy Bind-Off, go to http://www.knitty.com /ISSUEfall09/FEATjssbo.php.*

Instructions

Using the Möbius strip method, CO 170 sts. Spread the sts around the needles, laying the needle down on a flat surface to ensure that the sts lie parallel on the cables and that the needle overlaps only once. Place a marker on the RH needle for the beg of the rnd.

Rnd 1: Insert the needle through the slip knot and k1. Give the working yarn a tug to minimize any space between last cast-on st and first st of rnd. For the first half of rnd, sts are mounted alternately. Knit through the back loop of the next st, then the front loop of the following st around until the beg-of-rnd marker is hanging on the cable beneath your needle tips. You are halfway around. Notice the purl bumps along the needle where you have knit the first half of the rnd; once you knit a st on the 2nd half of the rnd, you will see 2 rows of purl bumps between your needle and the cable underneath. Knit to end of rnd.

Rnd 2: Purl.

Next 2 rnds: Knit.

Next 3 rnds: Purl.

Next 5 rnds: Knit.

Next 8 rnds: Purl.

Next 13 rnds: Knit.

Next 21 rnds: Purl.

Next 13 rnds: Knit.

BO kwise using Jeny's Super Stretchy Bind-Off.

Finishing

Weave in all ends.

Block the scarf to the finished measurements.

Hats & Mittens

Many of the projects in this chapter draw inspiration from popular hat and mitten styles throughout history. Whether you're looking for an easy project or something more challenging, you'll find patterns in this collection that you'll love to knit and wear. So break out your needles and get ready to cast on!

Finnish Päivätär
Hat and Mittens

Design by Heather Ordover

This set is named after Päivätär, goddess of the sun in the Finnish epic poem *The Kalevala.* Not only was Päivätär a goddess, she was a goddess of spinning, and her sister, goddess of the moon, was in charge of weaving. In this pattern you'll see the sun rise up the back of the mittens and ripples of color, like plies, cross the palms. The trellis pattern in the hatband and mitten gauntlet was used in both knitting and weaving. This design is based on traditional Finnish hats—the type you might see as part of a national costume—which were generally woven garments that were pieced and sewn together with longer than usual earflaps.

HAT

Size
Women's medium/large

Finished Measurements
Circumference at head: Approx 22"/56cm

Length (bottom of earflap to foldline): Approx 10"/25.5cm

Materials 🧶4
Brown Sheep *Lanaloft* (worsted weight; 100% wool; 160yds [146mm] per 3½ oz [100g]): 1 skein LL15S Roasted Pepper #006

Brown Sheep *Lamb's Pride* (worsted weight; 85% wool/15% mohair; 190yds [174m] per 4oz [113g]): 1 skein M140 Aran #095

Two size 8 [5mm] 24"/61.5cm or 36"/91.5cm long circular needles or size needed to obtain gauge

Size 000 [1.25mm] double-pointed needle (optional for I-cord)

Stitch markers

Split-ring stitch markers

Tapestry needle

Gauge
20 sts and 20 rows = 4"/10cm in St st.

Adjust needle size as necessary to obtain correct gauge.

MITTENS

Size
Women's average

Finished Measurements
Circumference around hand: 7½"/19cm

Length: 10"/25.5cm

Note: To fit a 7"/18cm palm circumference and a 7¾"/19.5cm long woman's hand (measuring from base of palm to tip of longest finger).

Materials
The March Hare worsted, 100% wool, 100g/3.5oz, 440yds/402m, Cream (MC), 1 skein

The March Hare silk blend, 70% merino/30% silk, 100g/3.5oz, 435yds /398m, Scarlet Letter (CC), 1 skein

Size 0 [2mm] 24"/61cm and 36"/91.5cm circular needles or size needed to obtain gauge

Stitch markers

Tapestry needle

Gauge
34 sts and 37 rows = 4"/10cm in St st.

Adjust needle size as necessary to obtain correct gauge.

Pattern Notes

Construction: In order to have a continuous plaited border to the hat, "extra" stitches have to be counted in to create the vertical edges of the earflaps. From the beginning of the round, the first earflap will require 40 stitches, the back of the hat will use 30 stitches, the second earflap will use 40 stitches, and the front of the hat will use the remaining 50 stitches. This is also why knitting on two circular needles is useful for this hat—the number of stitches is quite large at the outset but decreases markedly once the earflaps are complete. The earflaps have a "center line" of paired decreases and matching edge decreases that "seam" the earflap to the plaited border. This construction, when complete, will leave a total of 14 stitches remaining at the top of the earflap, which is now the lower edge of the hatband proper.

HAT INSTRUCTIONS

To CO, loosely knot MC and CC1 around one circular needle. Do not count this st in your CO.

Hold the CC over your index finger and the MC over your thumb. This will give you two separate rows of color for your CO edge.

Using the long-tail method and the two colors, CO 160 sts. Using two circular needles, distribute sts evenly and join carefully in the round, making sure not to twist sts.

Plaited Edge

Note: The plaited edge will roll. Depending on your process, let that roll determine your "right" and "wrong" side (or red or white dominant side). The sample you see here has a dominant red side as the "right" side, and thus a red bonnet in back.

Rnd 1: With yarns in back, k1 MC, k1 CC around (end with CC).

Rnd 2: Bring yarns to front, p1 MC, p1 CC around, keeping yarn in front and bringing working yarn over the top of the previous color.

Rnd 3: Keep yarns in front, p1 MC, p1 CC, bringing working yarn under previous color.

Optional Rep: Rnds 1–3 once.

Rnd 4: Bring yarns to back, then [k1 MC, k1 CC] around.

Earflap

At start of rnd, pm, count 40 sts and place the split-ring marker. This is where the first earflap will end when the decs are complete. Skip next 30 sts for the back, pm, count 40 sts and place another split-ring marker. This is where the second earflap will end when the decs are complete. The rem 50 sts are the front sts.

First Earflap

Row 1 (RS): K24.

Row 2 (WS): Sl 1 wyif, p5.

Row 3: Sl 1, ssk, k2tog, k2, ssk.

Row 4: Sl 1 wyif, p6, p2tog.

Row 5: Sl 1, k7, ssk.

Row 6: Sl 1 wyif, p8, p2tog.

Row 7: Sl 1, k2, ssk, k2tog, k3, ssk.

Row 8: Sl 1 wyif, p8, p2tog.

Row 9: Sl 1, k2, ssk, k2tog, k3, ssk.

Row 10: Sl 1 wyif, p8, p2tog.

Row 11: Sl 1, k2, ssk, k2tog, k4.

Row 12: Sl 1 wyif, p9.

Row 13: Sl 1, k10.

Row 14: Sl 1 wyif, p11.

Row 15: Sl 1, k3, ssk, k2tog, k4, ssk.

Row 16: Sl 1 wyif, p10, p2tog.

Row 17: Sl 1, k11, ssk.

Row 18: Sl 1 wyif, p12, k2tog.

Row 19: Sl 1, k4, ssk, k2tog, k5, ssk.

Row 20: Sl 1 wyif, p9, k1, p2, k2tog.

Place 14 sts on a holder.

Second Earflap

Work same as First Earflap.

Body

There should be 108 sts on the rnd—14 sts earflap, 50 sts front, 14 sts earflap, 30 sts back. Knit Rnds 1–24 foll 36-st rep Hat Chart A, pm after each 36 sts and rep sts 1–36 three times to create the entire, continuous front band.

Crown

Set-up Rnd: Using MC only, purl around, pm every 12 sts (9 sections total).

Rnd 1: *Knit to 2 sts before marker, k2tog; rep from * around.

Rnd 2: Knit.

Rnds 3–6: *Knit to 2 sts before marker, k2tog; rep from * around.

Rnd 7: Knit.

Rnds 8–12: *Knit to 2 sts before marker, k2tog rep from * around.

Rnd 13: Knit.

Rnd 14: *Knit to 2 sts before marker, k2tog; rep from * around.

Rnd 15: K2tog around—9 sts.

Break yarn, leaving an 8"/20.5cm tail.

With tapestry needle, thread tail through rem 9 sts and pull tight. Secure tail on WS.

Finishing

Weave in all ends and block as necessary.

FINNISH PÄIVÄTÄR HAT CHART

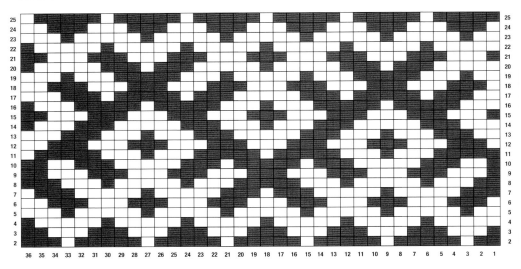

FINNISH PÄIVÄTÄR HAT EARFLAP CHART

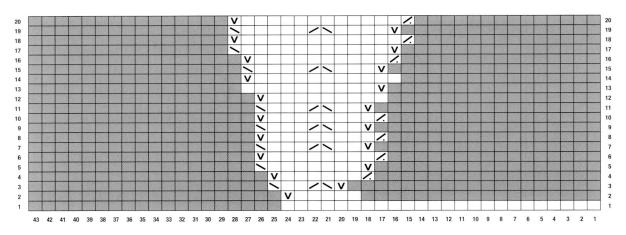

MITTENS INSTRUCTIONS

Loosely knot MC and CC1 around one circular needle. *Do not count this st in your CO.* Hold the CC over your index finger and the MC over your thumb. This will give you two separate rows of color for your CO edge. Using the long-tail method and the two colors, CO 80 sts. PM for beg of rnd and join, taking care not to twist sts.

Plaited Edge

Note: The plaited edge will roll. Depending on your process, let that roll determine your "right" and "wrong" side (or red or white dominant side). The sample you see here has a dominant red side as the "right" side, and thus a red bonnet in back.

Rnd 1: With yarns in back, k1 MC, k1 CC around (end with CC).

Rnd 2: Bring yarns to front, p1 MC, p1 CC around, keeping yarn in front and bringing working yarn over the top of the previous color.

Rnd 3: Keep yarns in front, p1 MC, p1 CC, bringing working yarn under previous color.

Optional Rep: Knit Rnds 1–3 once.

Rnd 4: Bring yarns to back, then [k1 MC, k1 CC] around. **Optional:** For a very neat edge, use this rnd to pick up the CO sts one at a time to knit tog with the sts on the needle to create a more solid "tube" of plaiting.

Gauntlet, Hand, and Thumb

Follow Gauntlet Chart B. (**Note:** Row 35 is the dec rnd.) Knit in pat, using black boxes indicated as the insert site for thumb gussets. Foll Hand/Thumb Chart C, inserting right and left thumb gussets as appropriate. Cont gusset incs to row indicated by the top of each black box. Place thumb sts onto a holder or waste yarn when knitting first complete rnd after black boxes are complete. CO 4 sts to replace thumb gusset sts.

Knit to Row 58 to begin hand decs. Dec as indicated on chart, every row, paired decs leaning into middle of mitten. When 8 sts are left (4 border sts and 4 center sts) on each side, BO with Kitchener stitch as you would with a sock toe. Alternately, use a three-needle BO with the mitten pulled inside out.

Place thumb sts on needle, pick up 12 sts to form the "inside" of the thumb. **Note:** Two different pattern choices are shown. The sample was knitted with the pattern that continues the edge pattern, making a virtually invisible thumb when mitten is flat.

Once sts are picked up, begin thumb with Rnd 22 and foll the appropriate thumb chart. Use Kitchener stitch to close.

Finishing

Weave in all ends.

Turn mitten right side out, block lightly.

Pattern Notes

If you are at all concerned about making two left-thumbed mittens rather than a pair with the thumbs in the correct place, you may wish to knit two at a time on the circular needles. This pattern lends itself well to either double-pointed needles or circular needles.

A larger size can be achieved by going up a needle size or two. Use your hand measurements and a gauge swatch to check. If that option won't work for you, either add or subtract the edge stitches that run up the outer edge of the mitten itself. For a more flared gauntlet, add one or more of the geometric bands of 2x2 color squares that run up the outer edge of the back of the mittens (column 174–181). These could be placed between two pattern reps throughout the gauntlets, indicating the outside edge of the hand. Those stitches could then become the same columns (column 174–181) in the hand pattern.

FINNISH PÄIVÄTÄR MITTEN GAUNTLETS CHART

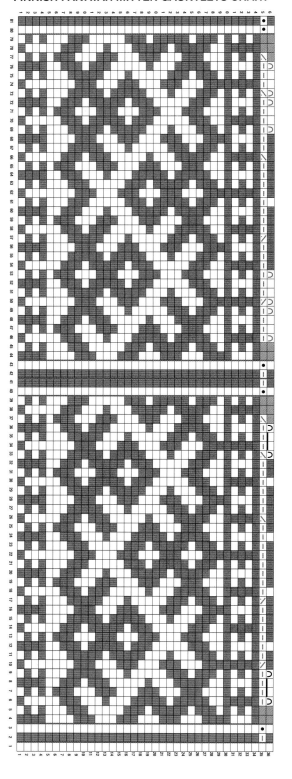

FINNISH PÄIVÄTÄR MITTEN CHART

KEY

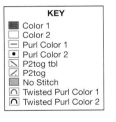

■	Color 1
□	Color 2
⊟	Purl Color 1
•	Purl Color 2
⦥	P2tog tbl
⦦	P2tog
▨	No Stitch
∩	Twisted Purl Color 1
∩	Twisted Purl Color 2

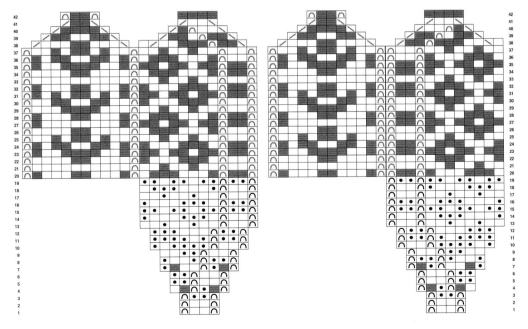

THUMB CHART

Winter Garden
Hat and Mittens

Design by Dawn Brocco

By inserting purl stitches into what would normally be a Fair Isle motif, this stunning set becomes a Bohus-inspired design. The purl stitches and a third color add texture and highlighting to the hat and mittens and make the motif sing. Garter ridges on the hat and mitten cuffs naturally form a turning row for the stockinette lining. I used a deep lining on the hat to add warmth around the ears, but a short lining on the mitten cuffs, where extra warmth isn't needed.

HAT

Size
Women's average

Finished Measurements
Circumference at head: Approx 20½"/52cm

Length (not including loops): Approx 8"/20.5cm

Materials ▨4▨
Cascade Yarns *Cloud 9*, (worsted weight; 50% angora/50% wool; 220yds [201m] per 3½ oz [100g]): 1 skein each Natural#101 (MC) and Navy #119 (CC1)

Cascade Yarns *Cascade 220 wool*, (worsted weight; 100% Peruvian wool; 164yds [150m] per 1¾ oz [50g]): 1 skein Bluebell #7816 (CC2)

Size 7 [4.5mm] 16"/40.5cm circular needle or size needed to obtain gauge

Size 7 [4.5mm] double-pointed needles

Sizes G/6 [4mm] or H/8 [5mm] crochet hook

Stitch holder

Stitch marker

Tapestry needle

Gauge
24 sts and 30 rows = 4"/10cm in St st.

21 sts and 24 rows = 4"/10m in charted pattern.

Adjust needle size as necessary to obtain correct gauge.

MITTENS

Size
Women's average

Finished Measurements
Circumference around hand: 7½"/19cm

Length: 7¾"/19.5cm

Materials ▨4▨
Cascade Yarns *Cloud 9*, (worsted weight; 50% angora/50% wool; 220yds [201m] per 3½ oz [100g]): 1 skein each Natural#101 (MC) and Navy #119 (CC1)

Cascade Yarns *Cascade 220 wool*, (worsted-weight; 100% Peruvian wool; 164yds [150m] per 1¾ oz [50g]): 1 skein Bluebell #7816 (CC2)

Sizes 6 [4mm], 7 [4.5mm], and 8 [5mm] double-pointed needles or size needed to obtain gauge

Sizes G/6 [4mm] or H/8 [5mm] crochet hook

Smooth waste yarn for provisional CO

Stitch holder

Stitch marker

Tapestry needle

Gauge
24 sts and 30 rows = 4"/10cm in St st with size 6 [4mm] needles.

21 sts and 24 rows = 4"/10cm in charted pattern with size 7 [4.5mm] needles.

Adjust needle size as necessary to obtain correct gauge.

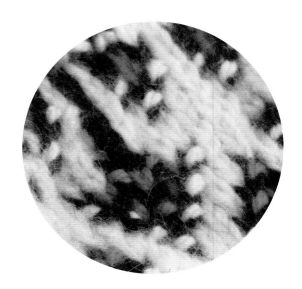

HAT INSTRUCTIONS

With MC and dpns, using long-tail CO method, CO 6 sts; divide evenly onto three dpns. Pm for beg of rnd and join, taking care not to twist sts.

Rnd 1: (K1, M1) 6 times—12 sts.

Rnd 2: (K2, M1) 6 times—18 sts.

Rnd 3: (K3, M1) 6 times—24 sts.

Rnd 4: (K4, M1) 6 times—30 sts.

Rnd 5: (K5, M1) 6 times—36 sts.

Rnd 6: (K6, M1) 6 times—42 sts.

Rnd 7: (K7, M1) 6 times—48 sts.

Rnd 8: (K8, M1) 6 times—54 sts.

Rnd 9: (K9, M1) 6 times—60 sts.

Rnd 10 and even-numbered rnds: Knit.

Rnd 11: (K10, M1) 6 times—66 sts.

Rnd 13: (K11, M1) 6 times—72 sts.

Rnd 15: (K12, M1) 6 times—78 sts.

Rnd 17: (K13, M1) 6 times—84 sts.

Rnd 19: (K14, M1) 6 times—90 sts.

Rnd 21: (K15, M1) 6 times—96 sts.

Rnd 23: (K16, M1) 6 times—102 sts.

Rnd 25: (K17, M1) 6 times—108 sts.

Rnd 26: Knit. Don't break MC.

With CC2 knit, inc 2 sts evenly on next rnd—110 sts.

Change to circular needle and pm at beg of rnd.

Purl 1 rnd. Do not break CC2.

With CC1, knit 1 rnd. Purl 1 rnd. Do not break CC1.

With MC, knit 1 rnd. Purl 1 rnd. Knit 1 rnd.

Foll 10-st rep of Winter Garden Chart for 21 rnds. Do not break CC1 and CC2.

With MC, knit 2 rnds. Purl 1 rnd.

With CC1, knit 1 rnd. Purl 1 rnd. Break CC1.

With CC2, knit 1 rnd. Purl 1 rnd. Break CC2.

Facing

With MC, knit 34 rnds (approx 5½"/14cm). BO.

Finishing

With tapestry needle, sew down facing inside hat, approx on the 2nd MC rnd, past the CC1 garter ridge. The CC2 turning ridge should lie flat around the hat's lower edge.

Top Chain Loops

Break a 2"/5cm long length of CC1 and CC2.

With crochet hook, leave a small tail and chain 18 with CC1.

Pull rem yarn end through last loop to end off. Rep with CC2.

Place both chains side by side.

Thread one group of yarn ends into tapestry needle and insert at top of hat to WS.

Thread other group of tails and insert into top of hat 1 st over from last insertion.

On inside of hat, double overhand knot both groups of ends, then double overhand knit them again. Pull snug and trim excess. Weave in all ends.

MITTENS

Note: The mittens are worked in two directions. The hand is worked from the crochet provisional CO down. Then the cuff is worked by picking up sts from the CO sts.

With smooth waste yarn, chain 46 sts, to allow enough room for picking up error.

With MC and size 6 dpns, pick up and k1 st into the back loops of the center 40 sts on the chain. Knit 1 rnd.

Thumb Gusset

Right Hand

Rnd 1: K3, M1, k1, M1, knit to end of rnd—42 sts.

Rnds 2–3: Knit.

Rnd 4: K3, M1, k3, M1, knit to end of rnd—44 sts.

Rnds 5–6: Knit.

Rnd 7: K3, M1, k5, M1, knit to end of rnd—46 sts.

Rnds 8–9: Knit.

Rnd 10: K3, M1, k7, M1, knit to end of rnd—48 sts.

Rnds 11–12: Knit.

Rnd 13: K3, M1, k9, M1, knit to end of rnd—50 sts.

Rnds 14–15: Knit.

Rnd 16: K3, M1, k11, M1, knit to end of rnd—52 sts.

Rnds 17–18: Knit.

Rnd 19: K3, M1, k13, M1, knit to end of rnd—54 sts.

Rnds 20–21: Knit.

Next rnd: K3, remove next 15 thumb sts to a stitch holder, CO 3 st onto right-hand needle, knit to end of rnd—42 sts.

Left Hand

Rnd 1: Knit to last 4 sts of rnd, pm, M1, k1, M1, knit last 3 sts of rnd—42 sts.

Rnds 2–3: Knit.

Rnd 4: Knit to marker, M1, k3, M1, k3—44 sts.

Rnds 5–6: Knit.

Rnd 7: Knit to marker, M1, k5, M1, k3—46 sts.

Rnds 8–9: Knit.

Rnd 10: Knit to marker, M1, k7, M1, k3—48 sts.

Rnds 11–12: Knit.

Rnd 13: Knit to marker, M1, k9, M1, k3—50 sts.

Rnds 14–15: Knit.

Rnd 16: Knit to marker, M1, k11, M1, k3—52 sts.

Rnds 17–18: Knit.

Rnd 19: Knit to marker, M1, k13, M1, k3—54 sts.

Rnds 20–21: Knit.

Next rnd: Knit to marker, remove marker, and move next 15 thumb sts to a stitch holder, CO 3 sts onto right-hand needle, knit to end of rnd—42 sts.

Main Mitten

Next rnd: Knit, inc 2 sts evenly—44 sts.

Knit 18 rnds (approx 6"/15cm from last garter st ridge rnd) or until desired length less 2"/5cm for fingertip shaping.

Top Decreases

Rnd 1: (K1, k2tog, k16, ssk, k1) twice—40 sts.

Rnd 2: Knit.

Rnd 3: (K1, k2tog, k14, ssk, k1) twice—36 sts.

Rnd 4: Knit.

Rnd 5: (K1, k2tog, k12, ssk, k1) twice—32 sts.

Rnd 6: Knit.

Rnd 7: (K1, k2tog, k10, ssk, k1) twice—28 sts.

Rnd 8: Knit.

Rnd 9: (K1, k2tog, k8, ssk, k1) twice—24 sts.

Rnd 10: Knit.

Rnd 11: (K1, k2tog, k6, ssk, k1) twice—20 sts.

Rnd 12: Knit.

Rnd 13: (K1, k2tog, k4, ssk, k1) twice—16 sts.

Rnd 14: Knit.

Rnd 15: (K1, k2tog, k2, ssk, k1) twice—12 sts.

Rnd 16: Knit.

Rnd 17: (K1, k2tog, ssk, k1) twice—8 sts.

Break yarn, leaving a 6"/15cm tail. Thread tail into tapestry needle and pull through rem sts. Tack down or after pulling the yarn through the sts, scoop under the st opposite the exit st, then find the nearest row of "ditches" or stitches, weave the tail down and up between the "bars" of each rnd for approx 1¼"–1½"/3cm–4cm, work back up in the opposite direction, going under where you went over previously, and over where you went under previously, for just two bars. Snip off excess.

Cuff

Unzip the crochet chain and place the 40 revealed sts onto the size 6 [4mm] dpns.

With CC2, knit 1 rnd. Purl 1 rnd. Do not break CC2.

With CC1, knit 1 rnd. Purl 1 rnd. Do not break CC1.

With MC, (k4, M1) around—50 sts.

Purl 1 rnd. Knit 1 rnd.

With size 7 [4.5mm] dpns, work 10-st rep of Winter Garden Chart for 21 rnds around for cuff. Do not break CC1 and CC2.

With MC, knit 2 rnds. Purl 1 rnd.

With CC1, knit 1 rnd. Purl 1 rnd. Break CC1.

With CC2, knit 1 rnd. Purl 1 rnd. Break CC2. With MC and size 8 [5mm] dpns, knit 5 rnds (approx ¾"/2cm) for hem. BO.

With tapestry needle, sew down hem inside cuff, folding on the 2nd MC rnd for turning ridge, past the CC1 garter ridge. The CC2 turning ridge should lie flat around the cuff's lower edge.

Thumb

Place the held 15 thumb sts onto 2 dpns. With MC and size 6 [4mm] dpns, pick up and k2 sts in left thumb corner, 1 st into each of the 3 CO sts, then 1 st in last corner—21 sts.

Next rnd: K14 sts, k2tog (to close the gap that inevitably forms in this corner), k to end of rnd—20 sts.

Knit 11 rnds (approx 1¾"/4.5cm).

Decreases

Rnd 1: (K2, ssk) around—15 sts.

Rnd 2: Knit.

Rnd 3: (K1, ssk) around—10 sts.

Rnd 4: (Ssk) around—5 sts.

Break yarn and end off as for fingertip shaping.

Finishing

Weave in all ends.

WINTER GARDEN MOTIF CHART

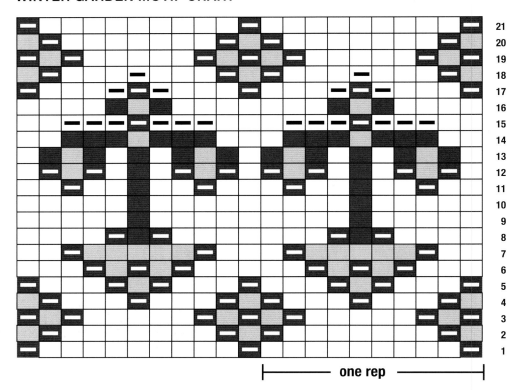

one rep

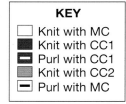

KEY

☐ Knit with MC
■ Knit with CC1
⊟ Purl with CC1
▨ Knit with CC2
⊟ Purl with MC

Icelandic Leaf Pattern
Tam and Mittens

Design by Hélène Magnússon

From the many different types of mittens in Iceland, it is the Leaf mittens from the West Fjords that inspired me to create these mittens and matching tam. The traditional mittens, as their name suggests, were decorated with a leaf pattern. The patterns featured different types of leaves, named *fimmtekinn* (fifth), *sextekinn* (sixth), *sjötekinn* (seventh), according to the number of row repeats required to create one leaf. I used much thicker wool for the Icelandic Léttlopi, worked rather tight, to make really warm and cozy mittens. The matching tam is a new take on the tradition and is sized following the same order as the mittens.

TAM

Sizes
Adult's small (medium, large)

Finished Measurements
Circumference at head: 19 (21, 23)"/48.5 (53.5, 58.5)cm

Diameter across top (can be blocked larger): 9½ (10½, 11½)"/24 (26.5, 29)cm

Materials 3 or 4
Ístex *Léttlopi* (aran weight; 100% pure wool; 109yds [100m] per 1¾ oz [50g]): 2 (2, 3) skeins Brown #0053 (MC); 1 skein White #0051 (CC1); 1 skein Turquoise #1404 (CC2); 1 skein Red #1409 (CC3); 1 skein Mustard #9264; 1 skein Black #0059 (CC5)

Sizes 4 [3.5mm] and 6 [4mm] double-pointed needles or size needed to obtain gauge

Stitch marker

Tapestry needle

MITTENS

Sizes
Adult's small (medium, large)

Finished Measurements
Circumference around palm: 8 (8¾, 9½)"/20.5 (22, 24)cm

Length: 9 (9½, 10)"/23 (24, 25.5)cm

Materials 3 or 4
Ístex *Léttlopi* (aran weight; 100% pure wool; 109yds [100m] per 1¾ oz [50g]): 2 (2, 3) skeins Brown #0053 (MC); 1 skein White #0051 (CC1); 1 skein Turquoise #1404 (CC2); 1 skein Red #1409 (CC3); 1 skein Mustard #9264; 1 skein Black #0059 (CC5)

Sizes 4 [3.5mm] and 6 [4mm] double-pointed needles or size needed to obtain gauge

Stitch markers

Scrap yarn for thumb markers

Tapestry needle

Gauge
20 sts and 28 rows = 4"/10cm in St st with size 6 [4mm] needles.

Adjust needle size as necessary to obtain correct gauge.

TAM INSTRUCTIONS

With smaller dpns and CC1, CO 96 (106, 116) sts; divide sts evenly on 3 dpns. Pm for beg of rnd and join, taking care not to twist sts. Change to MC and work 1 rnd in St st, then work in k1, p1 rib for 7 (8, 9) rnds. Change to larger dpns and St st.

Next rnd: (K4, M1) 24 times, k0 (2, 4)—120 (132, 144) sts.

Cont with MC only, work 4 (5, 6) rnds. Foll chart for Pattern A for 7 rnds. Foll chart for Pattern B1 (B2, B3) for 5 (6, 7) rnds. Foll chart for Pattern C for 7 rnds.

With MC only, work 3 (4, 5) rnds.

Crown

Rnd 1: *K2, k2tog; rep from * around—90 (99, 108) sts.

Rnds 2–4: Knit.

Rnd 5: *K1, k2tog; rep from * around—60 (66, 72) sts.

With MC, work 1 (2, 3) more rnd(s).

Follow chart for Pattern D.

Change to CC5 and work 1 rnd.

Decreases

Rnd 1: *K1, k2tog; rep from * around—40 (44, 48) sts.

Rnds 2, 4, 6, and 8: Knit even.

Rnd 3: K2tog around—20 (22, 24) sts.

Rnd 5: K2tog around—10 (11, 12) sts.

Rnd 7: K2tog around—5 (6, 6) sts.

Break yarn leaving a 6"/15cm tail; draw it through the rem sts.

With tapestry needle, thread tail through rem sts, pull tight and secure to WS.

Finishing

Weave in all yarn ends. Hand wash in lukewarm water with wool soap. Block tam to measurements on circular form (for example, a plate, or a piece of cardboard covered with plastic wrap). Allow to dry flat.

MITTEN INSTRUCTIONS

With CC1 and smaller dpns, CO 40 (44, 48) sts; divide sts evenly on 3 dpns. Pm for beg of rnd and join, taking care not to twist sts. Change to MC and work 1 rnd in St st, then work in k1, p1 rib for 7 (8, 9) rnds. Change to St st. Work 1 rnd with MC, then foll chart for Pattern A for 7 rnds. Foll chart for Pattern B1 (B2, B3) for 5 (6, 7) rnds. Foll chart for Pattern C for 7 rnds. Cont with MC only for 2 rnds.

Left Thumb

Next rnd: With MC, k12 (13, 15), k next 7 (9, 9) sts with contrasting scrap yarn for thumb, place sts back on left needle and k them again with MC, k to end.

Right Thumb

Next rnd: With MC, k1, k next 7 (9, 9) sts with contrasting scrap yarn, place sts back on left needle and knit them again with MC, k to end.

Main Mitten

Cont with MC for 21 (24, 27) rnds. Foll chart for Pattern D for 7 rnds.

Change to CC5.

Next rnd: *K20 (22, 24) sts, pm; rep from * once.

Top Decreases

Next rnd: *K to last 3 sts before marker, k2tog, k2, ssk; rep from * once—36 (40, 44) sts.

Rep last rnd until 8 sts rem.

Break yarn. Turn mitten inside out and join using three-needle BO.

Thumb

Remove scrap yarn and place the sts on the needles, picking up an extra st at each of the outer corners of the thumb hole—16 (20, 20) sts.

Cont with MC for 15 (17, 19) rnds. Change to CC1 and knit 1 rnd.

Change to CC5.

Next rnd: *K8 (10, 10) sts and pm; rep from * once.

Next rnd: *K to 3 sts before first marker, k2tog, k2, ssk; rep from * once.

Rep last rnd until 8 sts rem.

Next rnd: (Ssk, k2tog) twice—4 sts.

Break yarn, leaving a 6"/15cm tail.

With tapestry needle, thread tail through rem sts, pull tight and secure to WS.

Finishing

Weave in all ends. Close the gaps at the outer corners of the thumbs if needed.

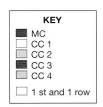

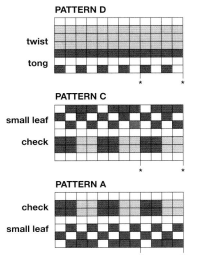

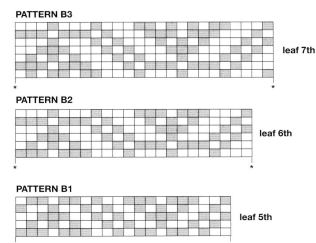

Aran Islands Teampall
Breachain Hat and Gloves

Design by Anne Carroll Gilmour

The design for this hat was inspired by a trip to Inishmore, the largest of the three Aran Islands that are nestled in beautiful Galway Bay on the west coast of Ireland. Because this trip was taken as a wedding anniversary celebration, I began with a knit knotwork version of my wedding band—a fifteen-stitch cabled border that is worked flat and then joined in a circle, to be picked up along the seed stitch edge and completed in the round. Because this design is all about Ireland, I used Irish yarns for the samples shown here.

HAT

Sizes
Adult's small (medium, large)

Finished Measurements
Circumference at head: 21 (22¼, 23)"/53.5 (56.5, 58.5)cm

Length: 8 (8½, 9)"/20.5 (21.5, 23)cm

Materials 🧶3

For Small Size: Black Water Abbey *Sportweight* (100% wool; 350yds [320m] per 4oz [100g]): 1 skein Bracken (MC)

Sublime Yarns *Kid Mohair* (sport weight; 60% kid mohair/35% nylon/5% merino wool; 122yds [112m] per 1¾ oz [25g]): 1 skein Blend Shade #0023 (CC)

Size 3 [3.25mm], 16"/40.5cm long circular needle or size to obtain gauge

Size 3 [3.25mm] double-pointed needles

For Medium Size: Black Water Abbey *Worsted* (worsted weight; 100% wool; 220yds [201m] per 4oz [100g]): 1 skein Grey Sea (MC)

Classic Elite Yarns *Inca Alpaca* (worsted weight; 100% baby alpaca; 109yds [100m] per 1¾ oz [50g]): 1 skein Viennese Teal #1167 (CC)

Size 4 [3.5mm], 16"/40.5cm circular needle or size to obtain gauge

Size 4 [3.5mm] double-pointed needles

For Large Size: Kerry Woollen Mills *Aran Wool* (worsted weight; 100% wool; 365yds [334m] per 8oz [200g]): 1 skein Jacob

Classic Elite Yarns *Inca Alpaca* (worsted weight; 100% baby alpaca; 109yds [100m] per 1-3/4oz [50g]): 1 skein Goucho Gray Heather #1176 (CC)

Size 5 [3.75mm], 16"/40.5cm circular needle or size to obtain gauge

Size 5 [3.75mm] double-pointed needles

For All Sizes:
5 markers

Cable needle

Tapestry needle

Gauge
For Small Size: 24 sts and 34 rows = 4"/10cm in St st with size 3 [3.25mm] needle.

For Medium Size: 22 sts and 30 sts = 4"/10cm in St st with size 4 [3.5mm] needle.

For Large Size: 20 sts and 24 rows = 4"/10cm in St st with size 5 [3.75mm] needle.

Adjust needle size as necessary to obtain correct gauge.

GLOVES

Size
Adult's small (medium, large)

Finished Measurements
Circumference around palm: 8 (9, 9½)"/20.5 (23, 24)cm

Length: 10 (10½, 11)"/25.5 (26.5, 28)cm

Materials 🧶1

For Small Size: Black Water Abbey *Sportweight* (100% wool; 350yds [320m] per 4oz [100g]): 1 skein Bracken (MC)

Size 3 [3.25mm], double-pointed needle or size to obtain gauge

For Medium Size: Black Water Abbey *Worsted* (100% wool; 220yds [201m] per 4oz [100g]): 1 skein Grey Sea (MC)

Size 4 [3.5mm], 16"/40.5cm circular needle or size to obtain gauge

For Large Size: Kerry Woollen Mills *Aran Wool* (worsted weight; 100% wool; 365yds [334m] per 8oz [200g]): 1 skein Jacob

Size 5 [3.75mm], 16"/40.5cm circular needle or size to obtain gauge

For All Sizes:
Cable needle

Crochet hook

3 small stitch holders

4 larger stitch holders

Tapestry needle

Pattern Notes
This pattern is for experienced knitters with good chart reading skills and an understanding of open/closed (aka knotwork) cable construction, picot hems, and reverse grafting. Because of the textural complexity of this design, the three sizes are obtained by changing gauge for each size. This hat is worked with a knotwork border, which is knit flat, joined in a ring, then picked up and knit vertically.

Special Techniques
KBB (Knit back backward): Used only on knotwork cable bases as an alternative to turning and purling back for the few stitches involved—a very handy technique for this type of open and closed knotwork cable knitting.

Border

With MC, CO 15 sts on one dpn (use a provisional CO) and leave an extra 20"/51cm tail to graft join when border is complete. Work back and forth foll Hat Border Chart #1 for 5 complete repeats of the 36-row chart.

Join: Using K&P grafting in pat as est, invisibly graft completed hat border live st end to CO end, with RS facing you to form a ring. **Note:** This join will mark the beg of each rnd. (This ring may look large; however, the next pick-up rnd takes it in.)

Pick-up Rnd on Lower Edge: Using circular needle with RS of knot border ring facing you, start just above your join by sliding the needle tip under all the purl bumps around one Seed st edge. There should be about 90–92 sts on needle. Pm at joining and knit 1 rnd into your picked up sts; at the same time evenly pick up enough extra sts to total 100 sts. (**Important Note:** The goal here with pat placement is to line up 20 sts above each triple knot section of the border, so approx 1 extra st after every 9th st or so.)

P 1 rnd, k 1 rnd, p 1 rnd for Garter st.

Hat Top Chart: K 1st st tbl after rnd marker, p19, *pm, k1tbl, p19*; rep from * to * to end of rnd.

Foll Chart #2, working 20 sts at each marker (5 reps per rnd) from Rnd 1–34 (note that on Rnd 34 you will have to k2tog tbl to get to the final 5 sts).

Break off yarn, leaving a 20"/51cm tail to draw through these 5 sts and finish top with a 16-st crochet chain loop, lashing the final tail firmly several times around the base of this loop, or anchor rem tail firmly inside hat.

Hem Edge Border

Work as for pick-up rnd on lower edge.

P 1 rnd, k 1 rnd, p 1 rnd for Garter st.

K 3 rnds.

Picot Rnd: *Yo, k2tog; rep from * to end of rnd.

Hem Facing: K 3 rnds.

Break off yarn and weave tail on the last rnd.

Turn and Tack Hem

Turn the live st edge up behind your work, purl sides tog (it will fold nicely along the line of picot sts), and carefully catch the first st with its corresponding inside st and knit these tog (**do not BO**), then the 2nd live st with the 2nd st and so forth to the end of rnd, taking care to cont working st for st. If you offset any sts, your hem will twist unattractively. **Note:** Check before you cont to make sure you are back to the original 100 sts.

Liner

K even for another 3 (3.25, 3.5)"/7.5 (8.25, 9) cm more for inner liner. Beak off yarn, leaving a 60"/150cm tail. Thread tapestry needle and invisibly whipstitch the live liner sts to the upper inside edge of the border, being careful to keep the liner straight. **Note:** From the inside you can see where each wedge section begins and ends, so place each 20th st between each section. Turning the project inside out can make this easier. This finish works better than whip stitching a BO edge because the fabric maintains good flexibility.

Finishing

Weave in all ends. Gently rinse and squeeze out any excess moisture. Block over a medium-size bowl or pot.

Cuff Border

With MC, CO 15 sts on one dpn (use a provisional CO) and leave an extra 20"/51cm tail to graft join when border is complete. Then with 2nd dpn, work back and forth foll Cuff Double-Knot Border Chart #1 for two complete repeats of the 36-row chart.

Join: Using K&P grafting in pat as est, invisibly graft completed hat border live st end to CO end, with RS facing you to form a ring. **Note:** This join will mark the beg of each rnd.

Pick-up Rnd on Lower Edge: Using circular needle with RS of knot border ring facing you, start just above your join by sliding the needle tip under all the purl bumps around one Seed st edge. You should have about 32 sts on the needle. Pm at joining and knit 1 rnd into your picked up sts; at the same time evenly pick up enough extra sts to total 40 sts.

P 1 rnd, k 1 rnd, p 1 rnd for Garter st.

Turned Picot Hem

K 3 rnds.

Picot Rnd: *Yo, k2tog; rep from * to end of rnd.

Hem Facing: K 3 rnds.

Turn and Tack Hem

Turn the live st edge up behind your work, purl sides tog (it will fold nicely along the line of picot sts), and carefully catch the first st with its corresponding inside st and knit these tog **(do not BO)**, then the 2nd live st with the 2nd st and so forth to the end of rnd, taking care to cont working st for st. If you offset any sts, your hem will twist unattractively. **Note:** Check before you cont to make sure you are back to the original 40 sts.

Tip: You can slide an empty dpn under the inside cuff sts. This will help keep your hem from twisting, and you can use a third dpn to do the BO as in a standard third-needle BO.

Pattern Notes

This pattern is for experienced knitters who like texture, understand open/closed (aka knotwork) cable construction, and are good chart readers. Please note that instructions that apply only to the left hand are highlighted in **bold**; those for the right hand are in *italics*. All normal text applies to both hands.

These gloves are worked with a knotwork cuff border, which is knit flat, joined in a ring, then picked up and knit vertically.

Special Techniques

KBB (Knit back backward): Used only on knotwork cable bases as an alternative to turning and purling back for the few stitches involved—a very handy technique for this type of open and closed knotwork cable knitting.

Hand Edge Pick-up Rnd: Holding cuff with RS facing you, begin pick-up around the rem Seed st edge just to the left of the grafted seam, exactly as for hem edge. Slide needle tip (but don't knit yet) under all the purl bumps around the edge, dividing evenly on your dpns. You should again have 32 picked-up sts. K into your picked-up sts; at the same time, evenly place enough incs to total 40 sts (inc after every 4th st).

P 1 rnd, k 1 rnd, p 1 rnd.

Note: You are now ready to est hand knot panel and thumb gusset base. Remainder of glove is worked mostly in St st except for pat sts indicated on hand knot panel chart.

Hand Knot Set-up Panel:

Needle #1: Using Needle #1 (all hand knot panel sts will go on Needle #1), k2, pm on needle to indicate beg of Hand Tri-ring Knot Chart, p11, pm on needle to indicate end of Knot Chart panel chart, k2—15 sts on Needle #1.

For Left Hand Only:

Needle #2: K15.

Needle #3 (set up thumb gusset as foll):

K7, pm on needle to indicate beg of thumb gusset, k a right raised inc, k1, k a left raised inc, pm to indicate end of thumb gusset, k2—12 sts on Needle #3 (this will inc by 2 sts every 4th rnd to the end of the thumb gusset).

For Right Hand Only:

Needle #2 (set up thumb gusset as foll):

K2, pm on needle to indicate beg of thumb gusset, k a right raised inc, k1, k a left raised inc,

pm on needle to indicate end of thumb gusset, k7—12 sts on Needle #2 (this number will inc by 2 sts every 4th rnd to end of the thumb gusset).

Needle #3: K15.

Beg following Knot Chart on Needle #1 at Rnd 1, then cont around for 3 rounds even as est.

On next (4th) rnd rep thumb gusset incs as indicated below:

Thumb Gusset Incs on Needle #2 for Right Hand; *on Needle #3 for Left Hand.*

Work as est to first gusset marker, sm, work a right lifted inc, k to second gusset marker, work a left lifted inc, sm—2 sts inc.

Cont working in this manner, completing each rnd of the Hand Knot Chart; at the same time, work the thumb gusset incs as described above on every 4th round (indicated by asterisks on chart) until there are 15 sts between the two thumb gusset markers.

Cont to work even until thumb gusset reaches desired length to base of the glove's thumb (2–4 more rnds or so).

On next rnd, work even as est to first thumb gusset marker, then set aside thumb sts as foll: Remove markers as you slide all 15 sts to holder or tie onto string to keep on hold until needed to complete the thumb.

CO 5 sts above thumb opening, then k rem sts of needle (this will change total st amount to 14 on *second needle for right hand* or **third needle for left hand**. Resume working as est until desired length to base of pinky (about 4–6 more rnds) or until Hand Knot Chart is completed.

Pinky

Work even as est all 15 sts on Needle #1, then for left hand only, using an empty needle, k first 12 sts on Needle #2 (slide the last 3 sts of Needle #2 onto Needle #3).

For Right Hand only, using Needle #2, k even across next 17 sts; then, with an empty needle k, the 12 sts rem from Needle #3.

Left and Right Pinkies

*Slide the 12 sts to the right end of the needle and with a second needle in your right hand, bring yarn across the back of the sts on left needle and k all 12 sts (as if making a really wide I-cord); rep from * 18–20 times or to desired length to tip of pinky.

K2 tog across 12 pinky sts—6 sts rem.

Twist crochet hook around bottom rung in the I-cord "ladder," hooking a st through all the ladder "rungs" to the tip of the pinky.

Break yarn, leaving a 6"/15cm tail. Thread tapestry needle with tail; draw tail through these rem 6 sts twice. Pull rem tail through to the inside, then lock tail into the fabric.

Main Glove

Reattach yarn and resume working hand in rnds over rem 32 sts. Beg with an empty needle, pick up and k4 sts at base of pinky (these 4 sts will become part of the ring finger—there are now 36 sts on needle); work across **next 4 sts from palm of Left Hand** or *next 5 sts from back of Right Hand.*

With another empty needle, work across next 12 sts.

With next empty needle, work next 11 sts as est.

With next empty needle, work across rem **5** or 4 sts, then also across the **8** or 9 ring finger sts (13 sts on ring finger needle—10 k sts and 3 p sts).

Cont even for 2 rnds over these 36 sts (remembering to leave the 11 p sts as est on back of hand); stopping just before starting the 13 ring finger sts. **Note:** You are now ready to start the ring finger, but first slide all but these 13 sts onto two holders or string, then proceed as foll:

Ring Finger

Work across the 13 ring finger sts as est, dividing these sts (5, 5, 3) onto three needles. CO 3 sts between digits sts before joining; then, with the fourth empty needle, work all 16 sts in-the-rnd, keeping the 3 back-of-hand p sts in pat as est for about 22–25 rnds or desired length to the tip of finger. **Note:** Try the glove on (carefully!) to see when fingers are long enough.

K2tog across all sts on every rnd until 8 sts rem at the fingertip.

Break yarn, leaving a 6"/15cm tail. Thread tapestry needle with tail and draw end through these 8 sts. Finish by invisibly weaving the end in securely as for pinky.

Note: You should now have the 23 sts rem on holder for palm and back of hand (8 of which are p sts).

Middle Finger

Reattach yarn and pick-up and k4 sts at base of ring finger; slide the 4 p sts next to the back of ring finger and the 5 k sts next to the palm side of ring finger off of the holders and onto two dpns. Keeping the 4 back of hand sts in p, work to the area between digits and CO 3 sts. Join in-the-rnd and work these 16 sts for 23–26 rnds or desired length (this is the longest finger on most hands).

Break yarn, then finish as for ring finger.

Index Finger

Reattach yarn and pick up and k2 sts at base of middle finger, then slide the rem 14 sts from holders; divide evenly onto three dpns. Work these 16 sts in-the-rnd as for other fingers, remembering to keep the 4 p sts at back of hand in pat, to desired length (about 22–25 rnds).

Break yarn, then finish as for ring finger.

Thumb

Slide 15 sts from holder onto two dpns, then reattach yarn and with another dpn, pick up and k7 sts at base of thumb opening (Needle #1—22 sts).

Dec Rnd 1: K to last st on third dpn, then ssk this st and first st from first dpn. K to before last pick-up st, then k2tog this last st with first st from second dpn—20 sts.

K 1 rnd even.

Dec Rnd 2: Rep Dec Rnd 1—18 sts.

K 1 rnd even.

Dec Rnd 3: Rep Dec Rnd [Decrease round 1]—16 sts.

K even for 17 rnds or desired length to tip of thumb.

K2tog on every rnd until 8 sts rem.

Break yarn, leaving a 6"/15 cm tail. Thread tapestry needle with tail and draw end through these 8 sts. Pull tightly and secure on WS.

Finishing

Weave in all ends.

CHART A: HAT BORDER

TOP

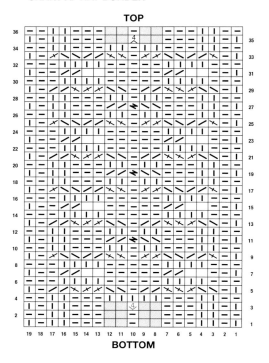

BOTTOM

Foll from bottom to top, R to L on odd numbered (RS) rows, L to R on even numbered (WS) rows.

15 sts (+ 4 then – 4 per rep) x 36 rows. Work 5 reps in total length, then after completing row 36 of 5th rep, work row 1 & 2, then join live st edge to CO edge. Remember that shaded blocks represent sts that have not yet been created or that have been decreased out.

Special note: On row 3, when this < 4 inc symbol appears, see first symbol at the top of chart key for cable base instructions.

CHART B: HAT TOP

TOP

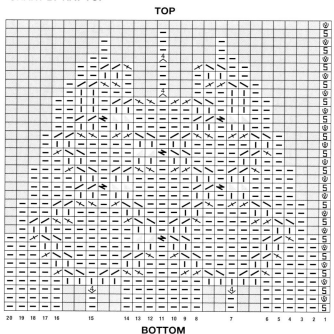

BOTTOM

Work this chart in the round, from bottom to top, right to left.

Note: On Rnd 33: P dbl dec thus: wyb, sl 2 as if to P, yf & P1, pass 2 sl sts over.

On final Rnd 34: K2tog tbl to end of rnd (only the 5 twisted knit chain sts will remain). 20 sts (+8 then -19 gradually to top) & 34 rounds, 5 repeats per rnd. Remember that shaded blocks represent stitches that either have not been created yet or stitches that once existed but have been decreased away. P2 tog decreases begin on rnd 10.

TEAMPALL BREACHAIN GLOVES CHART A: CUFF DOUBLE-KNOT

TOP

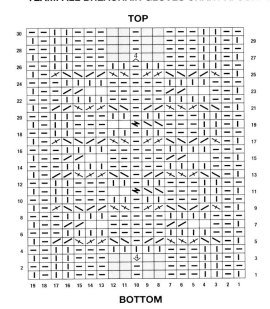

BOTTOM

Foll chart from bottom to top, R to L.

15 sts (+4 then -4) x 30 rows, worked flat for 2 complete repeats. Shaded blocks represent sts that have not yet been created or that have been decreased out.

GLOVES CHART B: HAND TRI-RING KNOT

TOP

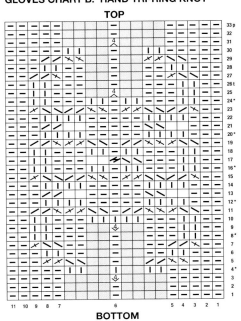

BOTTOM

Foll chart from bottom to top, R to L.

11 sts (+8 then − 8) x 33 rounds. Remember that shaded blocks represent sts that have not yet been created or that have been decreased out.

*= reminder—thumb gusset increases take place every 4th rnd until round 24.

t = reminder—set aside thumb sts within the next few rnds.

p = reminder—pinky starts here.

KEY

⤓   Make 4 into center st cable base inc by: work 1 lifted inc to the R of central st, K central st then work an L lifted increase, then using Kbb or short row (turn work), sl 1 (as to P if turning, as to kbb if not) kbb (or P if turned) 2 sts. Finish by (working right side again now if turning…) sl 1 as to k, work 1 lifted inc R, K center st, work 1 lifted inc L, K 5th st-cable base complete. (Center st changes back to P only after increases are complete & the cable divides, as indicated on chart—it just looks smoother this way, trust me) **KBB = Knit back backward** (very handy for knotwork cable bases, bobbles, entrelac knitting, & many other applications—highly recommended for this type of open & closed knotwork cable knitting).

Ⓥ   K through back loop (Ktbl).

[5]   With yarn at back, slip as to Purl (Wyb, sl as to P).

[I]   When working flat, K on right side, P on wrong side. In circular, K all.

[−]   When working flat, P on right side, K on wrong side, in circular, P all.

⟋⟍⟍   Twist 3 L by sl 2 to cn & hold in front, P 1, K 2 from cn.

⟋⟋⟍⟍   Twist 4 R by sl 2 p sts to cn & hold at back, K 2, p 2 sts from cn.

⟋⟍⟍⟍   Twist 4 L by sl 2 K sts to cn & hold in front, P 2, K 2 sts from cn.

⟋⟋⟍   Twist 3 R by hold 1 P st at back (w/cn or fingers) K 2, P held st.

⟋⟋◼◼   Cable 4 R by sl 2 sts to cn & hold at back, K 2, K 2 from cn.

◣◢◢⚡⟍⟍   Cable 4 L w/ P center by sl 3 sts to cn & hold in front, K 2, sl P st back to L ndl & P it, K 2 sts from cn.

⟑   Sl dec 4 sts thus: yb, sl 1st 3 sts as to P, K next 2 sts tog tbl, pass 1st 3 sl sts over st just made.

⟋⟋⚡◼◼   Cable 4 R w/ P center by sl 3 sts to cn & hold at back, K 2, sl P st back to L ndl & P it, K 2 sts from cn.

Turning Tides
Hat and Mitts

Design by Anne Carroll Gilmour

The charted designs for this New Zealand hat and mitten combo are inspired by Maori tribal traditional / symbols and patterns. With the movement of the ocean as its impetus, the waves in this pattern represent the cyclical yet ever-changing nature of life. In keeping with this theme, I chose shades that remind me of earth, sea, and sky.

HAT

Size
Adult's medium

Finished Measurements
Circumference at head: 22"/56cm

Depth from top of crown to cast-on edge: 8½"/21.5cm

Materials 🧶3 or 🧶4
Cascade Yarns *Cascade 220 Heathers* (worsted weight; 100% wool; 220yds [201m] per 3½ oz [100g]): 1 skein each #9446 Rust, #9454 Lt. Grape, #2448 Dk. Blue, #9338 Dk. Green, #2452 Lt. Green

Cascade Yarns *Cascade 220 Sport* (100% wool; 164yds [150m] per 1¾ oz [50g]): 1 skein each #8555 Black, #7807 Plum, #2404 Lt. Blue

Sizes 5 [3.75mm] and 7 [4.5mm] 16"/40.5cm long circular needles or size to obtain gauge

Sizes 5 [3.75mm] and 7 [4.5mm] double-pointed needles

Stitch marker

Tapestry needle

MITTS

Size
Adult's medium

Finished Measurements
Circumference at palm: 8"/20.5cm

Length: 9"/23cm

Materials 🧶3 or 🧶4
Cascade Yarns *Cascade 220 Heathers* (worsted weight; 100% wool; 220yds [201m] per 3½ oz [100g]): 1 skein each #9446 Rust, #9454 Lt. Grape, #2448 Dk. Blue, #9338 Dk. Green, #2452 Lt. Green

Cascade Yarns *Cascade 220 Sport* (sport weight; 100% wool; 164yds [150m] per 1¾ oz [50g]): 1 skein each #8555 Black, #7807 Plum, #2404 Lt. Blue

Sizes 5 [3.75mm] and 7 [4.5mm] 16"/40.5cm double-pointed needles or size to obtain gauge

Stitch markers

Tapestry needle

Gauge
22 sts and 34 rnds = 4"/10cm in St st with size 5 [3.75mm] needles.

20 sts and 32 rows = 4"/10cm in St st with size 7 [4.5mm] needles.

Adjust needles as necessary to obtain correct gauge.

Pattern Notes

This pattern is for skilled color knitters and good chart readers. There are never more than two shades per round, but there are frequent shade changes and long floats that should be locked back every fourth stitch. Hat is worked from bottom to top, mitts from cuff to knuckles. Charts are color-coded to correspond as closely as possible to Cascade 220 heathers and solid shades.

HAT INSTRUCTIONS

Using Black and smaller 16"/40.5cm long circular needle, CO 100 sts. Pm at beg of rnd and join, taking care not to twist sts.

Rnds 1–3: Work in k2, p2 ribbing around.

Change to larger circular needle and work four-color chain over next 3 rnds as foll (these 3 rnds count as Rnds 1, 2, and 3 as indicated on chart):

Chain Rnd 1: Attach Lt. Green and Lt. Blue. K 1 rnd alternating the two colors to end of rnd. (**Important Note:** Although this is the first of the 3 rnds, it winds up in the middle [as appears on charts].)

Chain Rnd 2: Attach Rust and Lt. Grape. Bring both yarns forward as if to purl (so they are hanging outside the circle). *Holding Rust in your left hand, p1, then p1 in Lt. Grape held by your right hand*; rep from * to * to end of rnd, always bringing Rust from below and Lt. Grape from above, so that the two yarns never twist or cross each other.

Chain Rnd 3: Now change hands and complete the chain by holding Rust in the right hand (above position) and Lt. Grape in the left hand (below position) and p1 rnd (Rust into previous rnd Rust sts and Lt. Grape into previous rnd Lt. Grape sts)—chain completed.

Cont to foll Hat Chart from Rnds 4–27 for main body of hat, then rep the 3 rnds of four-color chain as above (Chart Rnds 28–30). Resume Hat Chart at Rnd 31, working double decs as indicated until only 10 sts rem. K 1 rnd even.

Break yarn, leaving a short tail. Thread tail through tapestry needle and draw through rem sts, pull tightly, and secure WS.

Finishing

Wash and block over a pot, soufflé dish, or similar head-sized object.

Optional braid finish: Draw 12"/30.5cm tails from last three shades used through the final opening at the top, tie in a tight overhand knot close to the hat, and braid tightly for 2"/5cm. Add beads if desired, then tie a second overhand knot and trim and comb the yarn ends.

MITT INSTRUCTIONS

Using smaller dpns and Black, CO 40 sts; divide sts evenly. Pm at beg of rnd and join, taking care not to twist sts.

Rnds 1, 2 and 3: *K2, p2; rep from * to end of rnd

Work four-color chain over the next 3 rnds as indicated by chart Rnds 1–3 as foll:

Chain Rnd 1: Attach Lt. Green and Lt. Blue. K 1 rnd alternating the two colors to end of rnd. (**Note:** Although this is the first of the 3 rnds, it winds up in the middle [as appears on charts].)

Chain Rnd 2: Attach Rust and Lt. Grape. Bring both yarns forward as if to purl (so they are hanging outside the circle), *holding Rust in your left hand, p1, then p1 in Lt. Grape held by your right hand*; rep from *to* to end of rnd, always bringing Rust from below and Lt. Grape from above, so that the two yarns never twist or cross each other.

Chain Rnd 3: Change hands and complete the chain by holding Rust in the right hand (above position) and Lt. Grape in the left hand (below position) and p 1 rnd (Rust into previous rnd Rust sts and Lt. Grape into previous rnd Lt. Grape sts)—chain completed.

Rnds 4–26: Cont to foll Mitt Chart for left hand or for right hand from Rnds 4–20, then rep the 3 rnds of four-color chain as above (Chart Rnds 21–23). Change to larger needles and resume Chart at Rnd 24. Work as established until Rnd 26 has been completed.

Left Mitt

Rnd 27: Cont Left Mitt Chart over first 21 sts of Rnd 27 (back of hand sts), then work (1 black st, 1 background shade) alternating to end of rnd (palm sts).

Rnd 28: Beg thumb gusset incs as foll: Work to within last st of rnd, place first thumb gusset marker, k a right lifted inc in Lt. Blue, k1 Black st, k a left lifted inc in Lt. Blue (end of rnd marker will be second gusset marker).

Rnd 29: Work Rnd 29 as established, then rep paired thumb gusset incs in stripes as charted just after first marker and just before end of rnd marker.

Rnd 30: Work Rnd 30 as established.

Rnds 31–38: Rep paired incs as charted on all even numbered rnds to Rnd 38 (there are now 13 sts between gusset markers).

Rnd 39: Set 13 thumb sts aside as foll: Work as established to first gusset marker, remove marker as you slide all 13 sts onto a small holder for thumb, CO 1 Black st above thumb opening—40 sts.

Rnds 40–49: Cont as established.

Note: Stripes are done and color patterning resumes from Rnds 50–55 (as noted on chart).

Right Mitt

Rnd 27: Cont Right Mitt Chart as established over first 20 sts (back of hand sts), then work (1 Black st, 1 background shade) alternating to just before last st of rnd, (palm sts), then work st 40 as indicated on chart.

Rnd 28: Beg thumb gusset incs as foll: Work the first 20 sts of rnd as established, place first thumb gusset marker, k a right lifted inc in Lt. Blue, k 1 Black, k a left lifted inc in Lt. Blue, place second thumb gusset marker, k as established to end of rnd.

Rnd 29: Work even as established.

Rnd 30: Rep thumb gusset incs as charted just after first gusset marker and just before second gusset marker.

Rnds 31–38: Cont in this manner, with paired incs as charted on even numbered rnds to Rnd 38 (there are now 13 sts between gusset markers).

Rnd 39: Set aside the 13 thumb sts as foll: Work as established to first gusset marker.

Rnd 40–49: Remove markers as you slide all 13 sts onto a small holder for thumb, then CO 1 Black st above thumb opening and cont over the 40 sts as established from Rnds 40–49.

Note: Stripes are done and color patterning resumes from Rnds 50–55 (as noted on chart).

Both Mitts

On completing color charts, break off all shades but Black. Change to smaller needles.

Next rnd: *K8, k2tog; rep to end of rnd—36 sts.

Work in k2, p2 rib for 3 rnds. BO.

Thumb

Reattach Dk. Green and Black, pick up and k3 sts above thumb opening (1 Dk. Green/1 Black/1 Dk. Green), slide sts from holder to an empty dpn, then k 1st 2 sts from holder needle onto second needle; with third (empty) needle work across the next 8 sts from holder (front) needle, then slide the last 3 sts onto pick-up (back) needle and work across (8 sts now on each needle).

Cont to work thumbs in this three-needle circular technique as foll: K across all sts on front needle alternating the two shades as already established, then turn mitt and with third (empty) needle k across all sts on back needle.

Cont thumb in this manner with 2 more rnds Black/Dk. Green, then 4 rnds Black/Dk. Blue.

Next rnd: With Black only, *k2, k2tog; rep to end of rnd—12 sts.

Work in k2, p2 rib for 3 rnds. BO.

Finishing

Weave in all ends. Use loose ends to close any gaps or spaces at the base of the thumb if needed.

Hand wash gently and dry over a vase (or similar mitt-shaped object).

TURNING TIDES HAT CHART

TOP

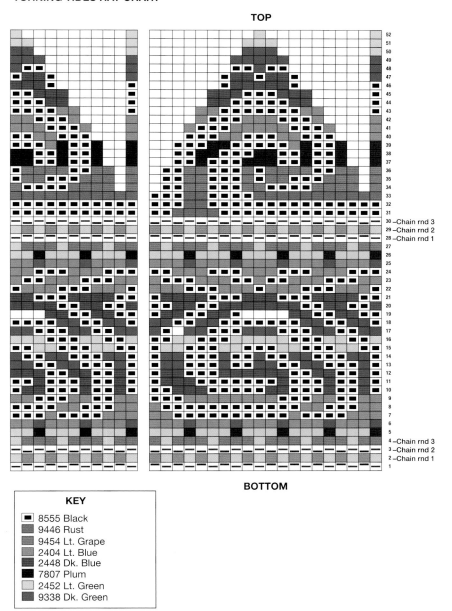

30 –Chain rnd 3
29 –Chain rnd 2
28 –Chain rnd 1

4 –Chain rnd 3
3 –Chain rnd 2
2 –Chain rnd 1

BOTTOM

	KEY
■	8555 Black
	9446 Rust
	9454 Lt. Grape
	2404 Lt. Blue
	2448 Dk. Blue
	7807 Plum
	2452 Lt. Green
	9338 Dk. Green

For both hat and mitts, foll charts from bottom to top, right to left.

Note on Charts: 20 sts x 53 rounds for 5 complete repeats. Chart is shown with 1 repeat & half of the following one to show positioning of double decreases (*dec rounds are also marked by asterisks), worked thus: Sl 2 as to K, K 1 pass 2 sl sts over. TIP: I find it easier to work the 1st of the 5 double decreases at the end of the round instead of the beginning (you will need to remove then replace the marker), as it eliminates the 1st & last st of the round—keep this in mind when knitting that 1st st. Shaded blocks represent sts that have been decreased away. Remember to carry long floats loosely across the back of work & lock back at least every 3rd st. Change to dp ndls when circle gets too small for circular ndl.

LEFT MITT CHART

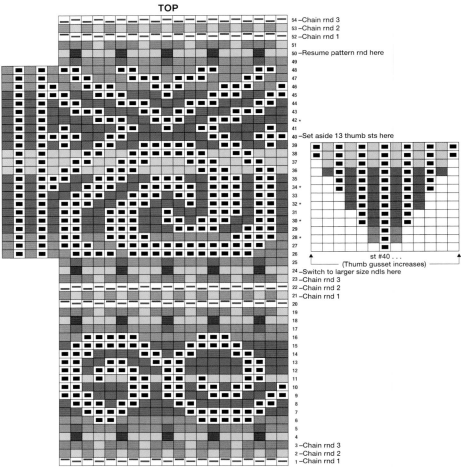

TOP

54 –Chain rnd 3
53 –Chain rnd 2
52 –Chain rnd 1
51
50 –Resume pattern rnd here
49
48
47
46
45
44
43
42 *
41
40 –Set aside 13 thumb sts here
39
38
37
36
35
34 *
33
32 *
31
30 *
29
28 *
27
26
25
24 –Switch to larger size ndls here
23 –Chain rnd 3
22 –Chain rnd 2
21 –Chain rnd 1
20
19
18
17
16
15
14
13
12
11
10
9
8
7
6
5
4
3 –Chain rnd 3
2 –Chain rnd 2
1 –Chain rnd 1

st #40 . . .
├── (Thumb gusset increases) ──┤

BOTTOM

KEY
■ 8555 Black
9446 Rust
9454 Lt. Grape
2404 Lt. Blue
2448 Dk. Blue
7807 Plum
2452 Lt. Green
9338 Dk. Green

Foll charts from bottom to top, right to left. Start cuff with 2 complete repeats for rnds 1–26.

1 x 1 black & background stripes on palm sts start after completing 1st 21 chart sts on rnd 27. Color patterning all around resumes after rnd 49.

*Reminder—asterisks at rnds 28, 30, 32, 34, 36, & 38 mark paired thumb gusset increase rnds.

Rnd 40 reminder—Set aside the 13 thumb sts on rnd 40 by working 1st 39 sts of rnd as indicated on chart, place next 13 thumb sts on holder, CO 1 black st & resume rnds as established over the remaining 40 sts. (FYI: Gray squares on thumb gusset chart represent sts that have not been created yet, to more clearly indicate the paired increases for the thumb gusset.)

RIGHT MITT CHART

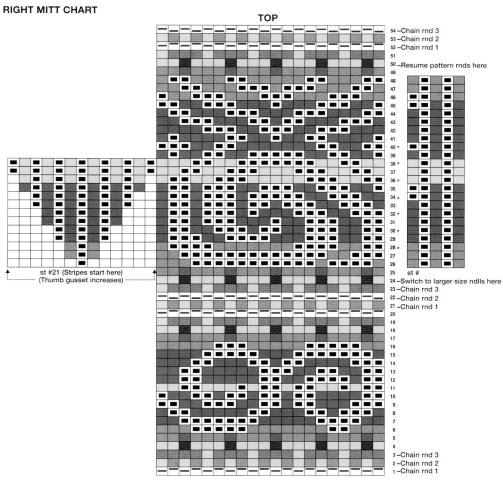

TOP

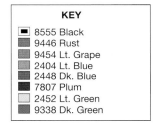

54 —Chain rnd 3
53 —Chain rnd 2
52 —Chain rnd 1
51
50 —Resume pattern rnds here
49
48
47
46
45
44
43
42
41
40 *
39
38 *
37
36 *
35
34 *
33
32 *
31
30 *
29
28 *
27
26
25   st #
24 —Switch to larger size ndlls here
23 —Chain rnd 3
22 —Chain rnd 2
21 —Chain rnd 1
20
19
18
17
16
15
14
13
12
11
10
9
8
7
6
5
4
3 —Chain rnd 3
2 —Chain rnd 2
1 —Chain rnd 1

st #21 (Stripes start here)
(Thumb gusset increases)

BOTTOM

KEY

- ■ 8555 Black
- 9446 Rust
- 9454 Lt. Grape
- 2404 Lt. Blue
- 2448 Dk. Blue
- 7807 Plum
- 2452 Lt. Green
- 9338 Dk. Green

Foll charts from bottom to top, right to left.

Start cuff with 2 complete repeats for rnds 1-26.

1 x 1 black & background stripes on palm sts (except last st of round, as noted above) start after completing 1st 21 chart sts on round 27.

Color patterning all around resumes after rnd 49.

*Reminder—asterisks at rnds 28, 30, 32, 34, 36, & 38 mark paired thumb gusset increase rnds.

T= Rnd 40 reminder—Set aside the 13 sts on rnd 40 by working 1st 20 sts as est, place next 13 thumb sts on holder, CO 1 black st above opening & resume rnds as est over rem 40 sts. (FYI: Gray squares on thumb gusset chart represents sts that have not been created yet, to more clearly indicate paired increases for the thumb gusset).

Japanese Sashiko
Hat and Mittens

Design by Janel Laidman

These Sashiko mittens and hat were inspired by the beautiful Sashiko quilting tradition of Japan. Sashiko quilting uses white thread to form intricate patterns on contrasting indigo cloth. Sashiko was used as a method to reinforce the cloth as well as form decorative patterning. Our mittens and hat have the same great contrast of indigo and white in a knitted form.

HAT

Size
Adult's medium

Finished Measurements
Circumference at head:
18"/45.5cm

Materials 🄲2🄲
Frog Tree *Alpaca Sportweight*
(sport weight; 100% alpaca; 230yds
[119m] per 1¾ oz [50g]): 1 skein
#000 White

Frog Tree *Alpaca Sport Melange*
(sport weight; 100% alpaca; 128yds
[117m] per 1¾ oz [50g]): 1 skein
#910 Blue

Sizes 3 [3.25mm] and 5 [3.75mm]
16"/40.5cm long circular needles or
correct size to obtain gauge

Stitch marker

Tapestry needle

Gauge
20 sts and 32 rows = 4"/10cm in St
st (blocked).

*Adjust needle size as needed to
obtain correct gauge*

MITTENS

Size
Adult's medium

Finished Measurements
Circumference at palm: 8"/20.5cm

Length: 10"/25.5cm

Materials 🄲2🄲
Frog Tree *Alpaca Sportweight*
(sport weight; 100% alpaca; 230yds
[119m] per 1¾ oz [50g]): 1 skein
#000 White

Frog Tree *Alpaca Sport Melange*
(sport weight; 100% alpaca; 128yds
[117m] per 1¾ oz [50g]): 1 skein
#910 Blue

Size 2 [2.75mm] double-pointed
needles or size to obtain gauge

Stitch marker

Tapestry needle

Gauge
32 sts and 36 rows = 4"/10cm in St
st (blocked).

*Adjust needles as necessary to
obtain correct gauge.*

HAT INSTRUCTIONS

Using smaller circular needle and Blue, CO 120 sts. Pm at beg of rnd and, join taking care not to twist sts.

Work in k1, p1 ribbing for 12 rnds.

K 1 rnd, inc 24 sts evenly spaced on rnd—144 sts.

Change to larger circular needle.

Join White and foll Chart 2, working shaping as indicated.

When Chart 2 is complete, break yarn, leaving a 6"/15cm tail.

Thread tapestry needle and draw yarn through rem 9 live sts, tighten, and secure to WS.

Finishing

Weave in all ends. Steam or wet block on 10¼"/26cm dinner plate.

MITTEN INSTRUCTIONS

First Mitten

Using White and dpns, CO 64 sts. Pm for beg of rnd and join, taking care not to twist sts.

Rnd 1: K.

Rnd 2: P.

Rnd 3: K.

Rnd 4: P.

Join Blue.

Rnds 5–16: Foll Chart 1 Rnds 5–16.

Rnd 17: P.

Rnd 18: K.

Rnd 19: P.

Rnd 20: K, inc 2 sts—66 sts.

Rnds 21–84: Foll Chart 1 Rnds 21–84; at the same time, at Rnd 44 create opening for thumb as indicated on chart (in red) by dropping working yarns and knitting indicated sts with waste yarn. Then drop waste yarn and cont working in pat with working yarns over waste yarn and into the rest of the rnd.

When Chart 1 is complete, close tip of mitten with Kitchener stitch.

Thumb

Return to thumb sts on waste yarn sts at the thumb opening. With White, carefully pick up sts above and below waste yarn on two needles, then snip waste yarn and remove it. When yarn is removed there are 22 live sts on your needles. Work these 22 sts in-the-rnd in St st with White until thumb is ½"/1.2mm less than desired length, then work as foll:

Rnd 1: *K1, ssk, k5, k2tog, k1; rep from * once—18 sts.

Rnd 2: K.

Rnd 3: *K1, ssk, k3, k2tog, k1; rep from * once—14 sts.

Rnd 4: K.

Rnd 5: *K1, ssk, k1, k2tog, k1; rep from * once—10 sts.

Close tip of thumb with Kitchener stitch.

Second Mitten

Work as for First Mitten, reversing colors (and working thumb in Blue).

CHART 1

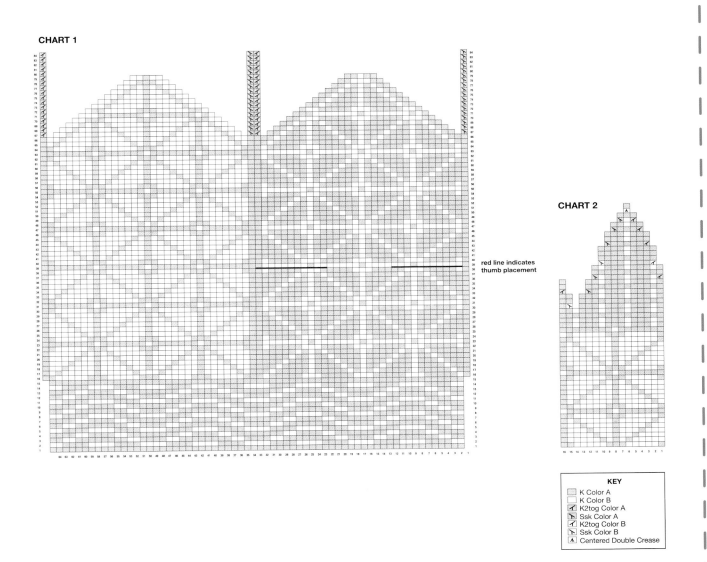

red line indicates thumb placement

CHART 2

KEY	
☐	K Color A
☐	K Color B
◢	K2tog Color A
◣	Ssk Color A
◢	K2tog Color B
◣	Ssk Color B
▲	Centered Double Crease

Fenceline Cap and Gloves

Design by Anne Carroll Gilmour

A vintage barbed wire collection from a little cowboy museum in Kemmerer, Wyoming, served as the inspiration for the Fenceline Hat and Mittens. The vast varieties of barbed wire available to ranchers around the turn of the last century offered an array of simple but bold linear patterns that seemed to shout "knit me!" Although this is fairly easy Fair Isle–type colorwork (there are no long floats and no more than two shades per round), good two-handed color knitting and chart reading skills are helpful when knitting this design.

HAT

Sizes
Child's medium/large (Adult's small, medium, large)

Finished Measurements
Circumference at head: 20 (21, 21¾, 23)"/51 (53.5, 55, 58.5)cm

Depth: 7 (7½, 8, 8½)"/18 (19, 20.5, 21.5)cm

Materials 🧶4
Recast as follows:

Brown Sheep *Nature Spun* (worsted weight; 100% wool; 345yds [315m] per 3½ oz [100g]): 1 skein each #601 Pepper (MC), #142W Spiced Plum (A), #522W Nervous Green (B), #124W Butterscotch (C), #225 Brick Road (D), #N59W Butterfly Blue (E)

Size 5 [3.75mm] and 7 [4.5mm] 16"/40.5cm long circular needles or size needed to obtain gauge

Size 7 [4.5mm] double-pointed needles

Stitch markers

Tapestry needle

Gauge
20 sts and 32 rnds = 4"/10cm in St st with size 7 [4.5mm] needles.

Adjust needles as necessary to obtain correct gauge.

MITTENS

Sizes
Child's medium/large (Adult's small, medium, large)

Finished Measurements
Circumference at palm: 6 (7½, 8, 9)"/15 (19, 20.5, 23)cm

Length: 10 (10½, 11, 11½)"/25.5 (26.5, 28, 29)cm

Materials 🧶4
Brown Sheep *Nature Spun* (worsted weight; 100% wool; 345yds [315m] per 3½ oz [100g]): 1 skein each #601 Pepper (MC), #142W Spiced Plum (A), #522W Nervous Green (B), #124W Butterscotch (C), #225 Brick Road (D), #N59W Butterfly Blue (E)

Sizes 5 [3.75mm] and 7 [4.5mm] double-pointed needles or size needed to obtain gauge

Stitch marker

Tapestry needle

Gauge
20 sts and 32 rnds = 4"/10cm in St st using size 7 [4.5mm] needles.

Adjust needles as necessary to obtain correct gauge.

Pattern Notes

To knit this hat with five colors instead of the "Black-top" variation shown here, eliminate the Black and use color A in its place. All other Hat samples are shown using only five colors; you will need an additional 75 yards or so of color A for the standard five-color version.

Fenceline Mittens in Sedona Spice colorway use the same materials (but not Pepper) and use the same chart as for the hat.

HAT INSTRUCTIONS

Using MC and smaller circular needle, CO 92 (96, 100, 108) sts. Pm at beg of rnd and join, taking care not to twist sts.

Rnds 1–3: Work in k2, p2 rib.

Change to larger circular needle and work a four-color chain over next 3 rnds as foll (break off MC as it won't be needed until chart is completed):

Chain Rnd 1: Join C and E, k 1 rnd alternating the two colors to end of rnd.

Chain Rnd 2: Join B and D, bringing both forward as if to p (so they are hanging outside the circle), *holding D in your left hand (below position) p1, then p1 in B (held by your right hand—above position)*; rep from * to * to end of rnd, always bringing D from below and B from above so that the two yarns never twist or cross each other.

Chain Rnd 3: Change hands and complete the chain by holding D in the right hand (above position) and B in the left hand (below position), then p1 rnd D into previous rnd D sts and B into previous rnd B sts—chain completed.

Foll 4-st rep of Chart for next 25 rnds. **Note:** Although there are no long floats, remember to carry yarn not in use loosely across back of work. Also asterisks at right of chart indicate thumb gusset inc rnds and do not apply to hat.

After completing Rnd 25 of Chart 1, rep the 3 rnds of 4-color purl chain exactly as at the beginning.

Crown

Reattach MC and cont with MC only.

K 1 (1, 2, 3) rnd(s), dec 2 (0, 0, 0) sts on first rnd—90 (96, 100, 108) sts.

Dec Rnd 1: *K 16 (14, 18, 16), k2tog, pm; rep from * to end of rnd, dec'ing 5 (6, 5, 6) sts—85 (90, 95, 102) sts.

K 1 rnd even.

Dec Rnd 2: *K to 2 sts before marker, k2tog, sm; rep from * to end of rnd dec'ing 5 (6, 5, 6) sts—80 (84, 90, 96) sts.

Rep Dec Rnd 2 every other rnd 4 times more—60 (60, 70, 72) sts.

Rep Dec Rnd every rnd until 5 (6, 5, 6) sts rem changing to dpns when necessary. Break off yarn, leaving a 6"/15cm tail. Thread tapestry needle and draw through rem sts, pull tightly, and secure to WS.

Finishing

Weave in all ends. Wash and block over a coffee can or similar head-sized object.

MITTEN INSTRUCTIONS

Cuffs

Using A and smaller dpns, CO 32 (36, 40, 44) sts. Pm at beg of rnd and join, taking care not to twist sts.

Rnds 1–3: Work in k2, p2 rib.

Rnd 4: Join D, working k sts only in D, p sts only in A to end of rnd.

Rnd 5: Join B, working k sts only in B, p sts only in A to end of rnd.

Rnd 6: Join E, working k sts only in E, p sts only in A to end of rnd.

Rnd 7: Join C, working k sts only in C, p sts only in A to end of rnd.

Rnd 8: Rep Rnd 4.

Rnds 9–11: Using A, work 3 rnds in k2, p2 rib.

Change to larger dpns and St st, foll Chart 4-st rep for 25 rnds; at the same time work thumb gusset incs as foll (**Note:** Thumb gusset inc rnds are indicated by *s on chart and are placed to make it possible to rem in color pat):

Thumb Gusset

Work even over 32 (36, 40, 44) sts for Rnds 1–8 of chart. Beg on the 9th rnd, sl rnd marker and work 1 lifted inc to the right, then place first gusset marker; k1, then work 1 lifted inc to the left; place second thumb gusset marker, k to end of rnd—34 (38, 42, 46) sts. Work 2 more paired incs on Rnd 10 of chart (1 right leaning after first marker, 1 left leaning before second marker). There will now be 4 thumb sts between the two gusset markers—36 (40, 44, 48) sts. Cont even in pat until you have completed Rnd 14; rep paired incs as above on Rnd 15. Work Rnd 16 even, rep paired incs on Rnd 17 (8 thumb sts between the two markers)—40 (44, 48, 52) sts. Work even in pat until you have completed Rnd 23. Rep incs on Rnd 24 (10 thumb sts between the two markers)—42 (46, 50, 54) sts. K last rnd of Chart even. Break off all yarn but A, then work 2 rnds even.

For size Large only: Work 1 more set of thumb incs (12 thumb sts between the 2 markers)—56 sts. Work 1 more rnd even.

Main Mitten

Next rnd: K1, place 10 (10, 10, 12) thumb sts on a small holder removing gusset markers; CO 2 sts above thumb opening—34 (38, 42, 46) sts.

Work 1 (1, 2, 2) rnd(s) even.

On next rnd, work mirror image decs above thumb as foll: K1, k2tog, k to within last 2 sts of rnd, ssk—32 (36, 40, 44) sts.

Work even until you are just past the tip of the mitten's desired length for the pinky.

Spiral Top Shaping:

Dec rnd: *K6 (7, 8, 9) sts, k2tog, pm; rep from * to end of rnd—28 (32, 36, 40) sts.

K 1 rnd even.

Next and all subsequent dec rnds: *K to 2 sts before marker, k2tog, sm; rep from * to end of rnd.

Rep last 2 rnds until only 12 sts rem.

Next rnd: K even.

Next rnd: K2tog to end of rnd—6 sts.

Break off yarn, leaving a 12"/30.5cm tail. Thread tapestry needle and draw through rem 6 sts twice, pull tightly, and securely to WS.

Weave in all ends.

Thumb

Pick up and k 2 (4, 4, 4) sts just above and to the right of thumb opening and with the 10 (10, 10, 12) sts from holder divide onto three dpns—12 (14, 14, 16) sts. Work even to desired length to tip of thumb (approx 14–18 rnds).

Next rnd: K2tog to end of rnd—6 (7 ,7, 8) sts.

Break yarn, leaving a 12"/30.5cm tail. Thread tapestry needle and draw through rem sts twice, pull tightly, and secure to WS.

Second Mitten

Work as for First Mitten but reverse spiral top shaping dec rnd as foll:

Dec rnd: *Ssk, k6 (7, 8, 9) sts, pm; rep from * to end of rnd.

Next rnd: K even.

Next and subsequent dec rnds: *Ssk, k to marker, sm; rep from * to end of rnd.

Complete as for First Mitten thumb.

Finishing

Weave in all ends.

FENCELINE INTERCHANGEABLE COLOR CHART

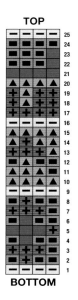

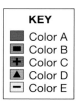

KEY	
■	Color A
◫	Color B
✚	Color C
▲	Color D
⊟	Color E

Follow chart from bottom to top, right to left. Asterisks indicate thumb gusset increase rounds.

Peruvian Ch'ullu Hat and Fingerless Gloves

Design by Elanor Lynn

As a child, my primary visual reference for Andean culture was Hergé's Tintin adventure *Prisoners of the Sun*. More recently, I've discovered the vast online textile collection of the Brooklyn Museum. These two *Ch'ullus* are inspired by an intricate contemporary example in this rich tradition. The original includes shells on the earflaps, woven chin ties, and a tassel. The fingerless gloves are worked with a solid-color palm, with the upper portion knitted in this rich traditional Andean style.

CH'ULLU

Size
Women's medium

Finished Measurements
Circumference at head:
23"/58.5cm

Length: 14"/35.5cm (without ties)

Materials ▨4▨
Cascade Yarns *Pure Alpaca* (worsted weight; 100% baby alpaca; 220yds [200m] per 3¾ oz [100g]): 1 skein each Red #3003 (A), Indigo #3025 (B), Ochre #3012 (C), White #3033 (D), Green #3019 (E), Magenta #3036 (F), Maroon #3047 (G)

Sizes 1 [2.25mm], 2 [2.75mm], 3 [3.25mm], and 5 [3.75mm] straight needles

Sizes 1 [2.25mm], 2 [2.75mm], and 3 [3.25mm] double-pointed and 16"/40.5cm long Circular needle

Tapestry needle

Gauge
34 sts and 38 rows = 4"/10cm in St st with size 5 [3.75mm] needles.

Adjust needle as necessary to obtain correct gauge.

FINGERLESS GLOVES

Size
Women's medium

Finished Measurements
Circumference at wrist:
6½"/16.5cm

Materials ▨4▨
Cascade Yarns <I>Pure Alpaca<I> (worsted weight; 100% baby alpaca; 220yds [200m] per 3¾ oz [100g]): 1 skein each Red #3003 (A), Indigo #3025 (B), Ochre #3012 (C), White #3033 (D), Green #3019 (E), Magenta #3036 (F), Maroon #3047 (G)

Sizes 1 [2.25mm], 2 [2.75mm], and 3 [3.25mm] double-pointed and 16"/40.5cm long Circular needle

Tapestry needle

Gauge
34 sts and 38 rows = 4"/10cm in St st with size 5 [3.75] needle.

Adjust needle as necessary to obtain correct gauge.

Pattern Notes

The hat is worked in multicolor intarsia/ stranded knitting. Due to the formidable number of ends to weave in for the seven-color version, you may wish to line your hat to avoid hours of finishing work. However, you then will lose the beauty of the stranding on the inside. Be sure to weave in the nonworking yarn when carried more than 4 sts. Also be sure to twist yarns at every color change. For the three-color version, since only two colors are used at one time, I've converted the pattern into round knitting. There is sufficient yardage to knit all three projects below.

When working charts, maintain pattern multiples, continuing pattern on any extra stitches.

THREE-COLOR *CH'ULLU* INSTRUCTIONS

With size 2 [2.75mm] dpns and A, CO 8 sts.

Pm at beg of rnd and join, taking care not to twist sts.

Rnd 1: Knit.

Rnd 2 and all even rnds through Rnd 22: Knit.

Rnd 3: Inc 1 st in each st—16 sts.

Rnd 5: Inc 1 st in each st—32 sts.

Rnd 7: Knit.

Rnd 9: (Inc 1 st in next st, k1) 16 times—48 sts.

Rnds 11, 13, 15: Knit.

Rnd 17: (Inc 1 st in next st, k2) 16 times—64 sts.

Rnd 19: (Inc 1 st in next st, k3) 16 times—80 sts.

Rnd 21: (Inc 1 st in next st, k7) 10 times—90 sts.

Change to size 3 [3.25mm] dpns or circular needle.

Rnds 23–26: With E and B, work Chart A, Rows 1–4.

Rnd 27: With B, inc 22 sts evenly across rnd—112 sts.

Rnd 28: With E, knit.

Rnds 29–43: With E and A, work Chart C, Rows 1–15 inc 8 sts evenly spaced within D sections on Rows 10, 12, and 14 of chart for a total of 24 sts inc'd—136 sts.

Rnd 44: With B, k1, inc 1 st in next 2 sts, k to last 3 sts, inc 1 st in next 2 sts, k1—140 sts.

Rnds 45–48: With B and A, work Chart A, Rnds 1–4.

Rnd 49: With A, inc 20 sts evenly across rnd—160 sts.

Rnds 50–94: Work Chart D with E and B.

Rnd 95: With E, k 1 rnd.

Rnds 96, 97, and 100: With size 1 [2.25mm] needle and B, knit.

Rnd 98: With B, k3, *with A, k3, with B, k3* end with A, k1.

Rnd 99: With A, k1, *with B, k3, with A, k3; rep from *, end with B, k3. Turn work so that you work the following rnd with WS facing.

Rnd 101 (WS): With size 5 [3.75mm] needles and B, BO 18 sts; with size 1 [2.25mm] needles k next 44; with size 5 [3.75mm] needles BO 35 sts; with size 1 [2.25mm] needles k next 44; with size 5 [3.75mm] needles BO rem sts.

Left Earflap

Row 1 (RS): Cont with size 3 [3.25mm] needles and B, k4; with E, k37; with B, k4—45 sts.

Row 2: With B, k4; with E and A, work Chart E, Row 1 over 37 sts; with B, k4.

Row 3: With B, k3, k2tog; with A and E, work Chart E, Row 2 over 35 sts; with B, k2tog, k3—43 sts.

Row 4: With B, k3, p2tog; with E and A, work Chart E, Row 3 over 33 sts; with B, ssp, k3—41 sts.

Cont as est, dec 2 sts every row until 9 sts rem.

Next row: Cont with B, k3, k3tog, k3—7 sts.

Next row (WS): Knit.

Next row: With E, k2; with B, k3; with E, k2.

Rep previous row, keeping nonworking yarn to the front of work.

Next row: With E, k3; with B, k1; with E, k3.

Rep previous row, keeping nonworking yarn to the front of work.

Next row: With E, k7.

K 63 rows.

Next row: K2, k3tog, k2—5 sts.

K 1 row.

Next row: K1, k3tog, k1—3 sts.

Next row: Knit.

Next row: K3tog.

Break yarn and draw through final loop.

Right Earflap

Rep as for Left Earflap.

Finishing

Sew short back seam to close BO edge. Close CO edge.

Weave in all ends.

SEVEN-COLOR *CH'ULLU* INSTRUCTIONS

With size 3 [3.25mm] straight needles and A, CO 10 sts.

Row 1 (RS): Knit.

Row 2 and all even rows through Row 22: K1, purl to last st, k1.

Row 3: K1, (inc 1 st in next st) 8 times, k1—18 sts

Row 5: K1, (inc 1 st in next st) 16 times, k1—34 sts.

Row 7: Knit.

Row 9: K1, (inc 1 st in next st, k1) 16 times, k1—50 sts.

Rows 11, 13, and 15: Knit.

Row 17: K1 (inc 1 st in next st, k2) 16 times, k1—66 sts.

Row 19: K1 (inc 1 st in next st, k15) 4 times, k1—70 sts.

Rows 21–24: With B and C, work Chart A, Rows 1–4.

Row 25: With C, inc 18 sts evenly across row—88 sts.

Row 26: With D, inc 1 st in next st, p to last st, inc 1 st in next st—90 sts.

Rows 27–36: With D, E and A, work Chart B, Rows 1–10.

Row 37: With D, knit.

Rows 38–41: With A and E, work Chart A, Rows 1–4.

Row 42: With E, inc 24 sts evenly across row—114 sts.

Row 43: With D, knit.

Rows 44–58: With D, E, F, and G, work Chart C, Rows 1–15, inc 8 sts evenly spaced within D sections on Rows 9, 11, and 13 of chart—138 sts.

Row 59: With D, k1, inc 1 st in next 2 sts, k to last 3 sts, inc 1 st in next 2 sts, k1—142 sts.

Rows 60–63: With F and B, work Chart A, Rows 1–4.

Row 64: With B, inc 20 sts evenly across row—162 sts.

Rows 65–109: Work Chart D with all colors.

Row 110: With D, k 1 row.

Rows 111, 112, and 115: With size 1 [2.25mm] needles and B, knit.

Row 113: With B, k4, *with A, k3, with B, k3; rep from * to end.

Row 114: *With B, k3, with A, k3; rep from *, end with B, k4.

Row 116: With size 5 [3.75mm] needles and B, BO 18 sts; with size 1 [2.25mm] needles k next 44; with size 5 [3.75mm] needles, BO 35 sts; with size 1 [2.25mm] needles k next 44; with size 5 [3.75mm] needles, BO rem sts.

Left Earflap

Row 1 (RS): Cont with size 3 [3.25mm] needles, with B, k4; with D, k37; with B, k4—45 sts.

Row 2: With B, k4; with all colors except A and B, work Chart E, Row 1 over 37 sts; with B, k4.

Row 3: With B, k3, k2tog; with all colors except A and B, work Chart E, Row 2 over 35 sts; with B, k2tog, k3—43 sts.

Row 4: With B, k3, p2tog; with all colors except A and B, work Chart E, Row 3 over 33 sts; with B, ssp, k3—41 sts.

Cont as est, dec 2 sts every row until 9 sts rem.

Cont with B, k3, k3tog, k3—7 sts.

K 67 rows.

Next row: K2, k3tog, k2—5 sts.

K 1 row.

Next row: K1, k3tog, k1—3 sts.

K 1 row.

Next row: K3tog.

Break yarn and draw through final loop.

Right Earflap

Rep for Right Earflap.

Finishing

Sew mattress st seam. Close CO edge. Weave in all ends.

Optional: Line with fleece.

FINGERLESS GLOVE INSTRUCTIONS

With size 1 [2.25mm] needles and B, CO 58 sts.

Row 1 (RS): Knit.

Rows 2, 5, and 6: Knit.

Row 3: With B, k4, *with A, k3, with B, k3; rep from * to end.

Row 4: *With B, k3, with A, k3; rep from *, end with B, k4.

Rows 7–11: Change to size 3 [3.25mm] needles. With C and B, work Chart A, Rows 1–5.

Row 12: With D, knit.

(**Note:** Sl sts to other end of circular needles so that you will be working one RS row after another RS row. Subsequently, all even rows will be RS rows and all odd rows will be WS rows.)

Rows 13–22: With D, A, and E, work Chart B, Rows 1–10. (**Note:** On Row 13, dec 1 st 1 st from beg of row—57 sts.)

Rows 23–26: With C and B, work Chart A, Rows 1–4. (**Note:** On Row 23, inc 1 st 1 st from beg of row—58 sts.)

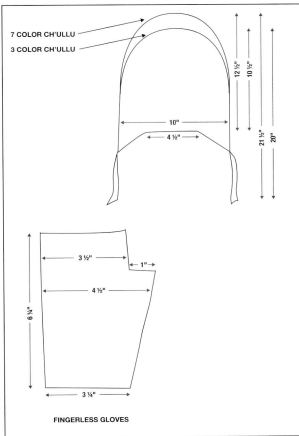

7 COLOR CH'ULLU
3 COLOR CH'ULLU

12 ½"
10 ½"
10"
4 ½"
21 ½"
20"

3 ½"
1"
4 ½"
6 ¼"
3 ¼"

FINGERLESS GLOVES

Row 27: With B, inc 14 sts evenly across row—72 sts.

Rows 28–43: With A, work in St st.

Row 44: K28, with size 5 [3.75mm] needle BO 15 sts, k28—57 sts.

Row 45: K1, p27, ssp, p26, k1—56 sts.

Rows 46–55: Work 10 rows even.

Row 56: Change to size 1 [2.25mm] needles. [K7, M1] 3 times, k14, [M1, k7] 3 times—62 sts.

Rows 57 and 59: K1, purl to last st, k1.

Row 58: [K7, M1, k1, M1] 3 times, k14, [M1, k1, M1, k7] 3 times—74 sts.

Row 60: With size 5 [3.75mm] needles, BO 44 sts.

Join Finger Openings

With size 1 [2.25mm] needle, pick up 3 sts from the middle point of BO edge (9th, 19th, and 29th sts).

Returning to sts on Row 60, (work three-needle BO on next st, BO 9 sts) 3 times, BO rem sts.

Break yarn leaving 14"/35.5cm tail.

Finishing

Sew mattress st seam. Weave in all ends.

CHART B

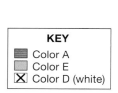

CHART A

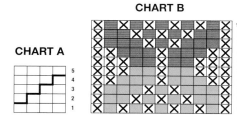

KEY
- Color A
- Color E
- X Color D (white)

CHART C

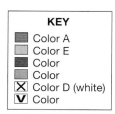

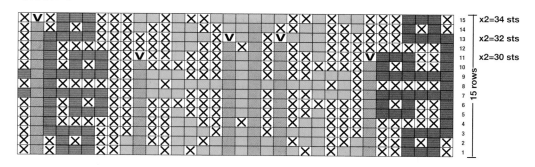

KEY
- Color A
- Color E
- Color
- Color
- X Color D (white)
- V Color

Full Repeat=56 sts on row 1 &
68 sts on row 15

(Only half each of pink and maroon motifs are shown.)

KEY

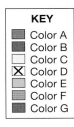

	Color A
	Color B
	Color C
X	Color D
	Color E
	Color F
	Color G

CHART D

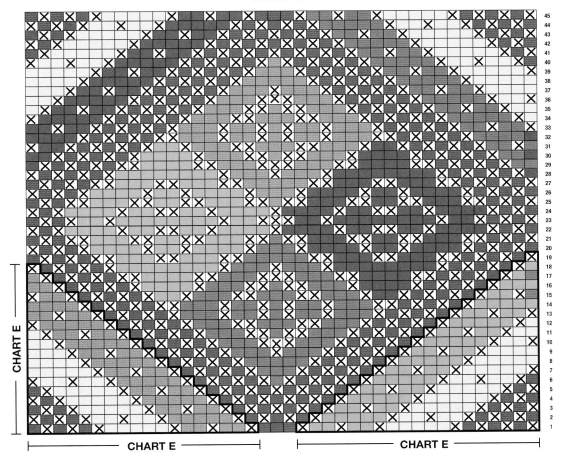

CHART E

CHART E

CHART E

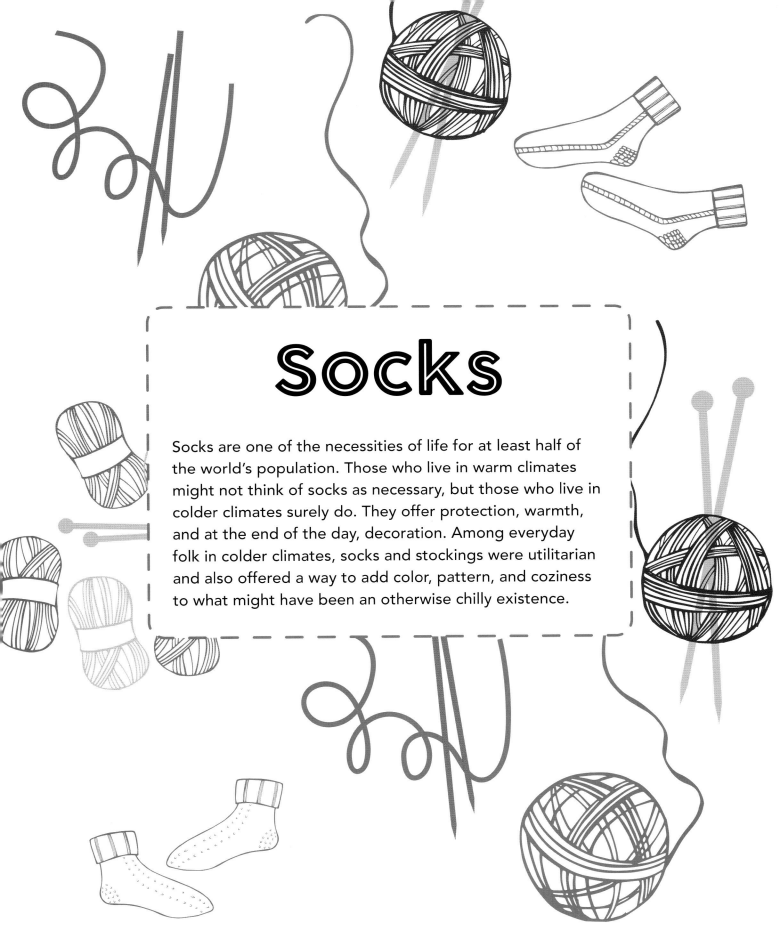

Socks

Socks are one of the necessities of life for at least half of the world's population. Those who live in warm climates might not think of socks as necessary, but those who live in colder climates surely do. They offer protection, warmth, and at the end of the day, decoration. Among everyday folk in colder climates, socks and stockings were utilitarian and also offered a way to add color, pattern, and coziness to what might have been an otherwise chilly existence.

Bohus-Style Peerie Socks

Design by Dawn Brocco

These socks combine Swedish Bohus and Scottish Fair Isle traditions. The corrugated rib is an element in the traditional Fair Isle style, whereas the leg motifs are Fair Isle peerie patterns, but by simply substituting certain stitches in purl, they become Bohus in style. Bohus-style knitting originated as a cottage industry in Sweden's Bohuslän province during World War II. Purl stitches worked into intricate colorwork patterns are a defining characteristic of Bohus designs, giving added dimension to the work.

Sizes

Women's small [US sizes 4–6] (medium [US sizes 6–9]; large [US sizes 8–11]). Instructions are given for smallest size, with larger sizes in parentheses. When only one number is given, it applies to all sizes.

Finished Measurements

Foot circumference: 7¼ (8, 8¾)" [18.5 (20.5, 22)cm]

Length from cuff top to lower heel: 7" [18cm]

Foot length: 9¼ (9¾, 10½)" [23.5 (25, 26.5)cm]

Materials 🧶4🧶

Cascade Yarns *Cascade 220* (worsted weight; 100% Peruvian wool; 220 yds [201m] per 3½ oz [100g] skein): 1 (1, 2) skein(s) Sand #9499 (MC); 13 (15, 17) yds [12 (14, 18.5)m] Flamingo Pink #7805 (D)

Cascade Yarns Cloud 9 (worsted weight; 50% merino/50% angora; approx 109yd [99.5m] per 1¾ oz [50g] ball): 13 (15, 17) yds [12 (14, 18.5)m] each Purple #147 (A) and Copper Brown #134 (B); 7 (8, 9) yds [6.5 (7.5, 8)m] Natural #101 (C)

Size 4 [3.5mm] double-pointed needles (set of 4) or size needed to obtain gauge

Size 3 [3.25mm] double-pointed needles (set of 4)

Tapestry needle

Gauge

24 sts and 32 rnds = 4" [10cm] in St st with larger needles.

24 sts and 28 rnds = 4" [10cm] over charted pat with larger needles.

Adjust needle size as necessary to obtain correct gauge.

Instructions

Cuff

With MC and larger dpns and using long-tail method, CO 44 (48, 52) sts in K1, P1 rib. Distribute sts evenly on 3 dpns; mark beg of rnd and join, taking care not to twist sts.

Rnd 1: [K1 A, p1 MC] around. Break CC.

Rnd 2: [K1 B, p1 MC] around. Break B.

Rnd 3: [K1 D, p1 MC] around. Don't break D.

Rnd 4: [K1 C, p1 MC] around. Break C.

Rnd 5: [K1 D, p1 MC] around. Break D.

Rnd 6: [K1 B, p1 MC] around. Break B.

Rnd 7: [K1 A, p1 MC] around. Don't break A.

Rnd 8: With MC, work in est rib around.

Leg

Rnds 1-2: Knit with MC.

Rnds 3-21: Work Chart. Break D.

Rnds 22-23: Knit with MC.

Heel Flap

Row 1 (RS): [K1, sl 1] 11 (12, 13) times, k1, turn—23 (25, 27) heel sts.

Rearrange rem 21 (23, 25) sts on 2 dpns to hold for instep.

Row 2: Purl.

Rep [Rows 1 and 2] 13 (14, 15) times—28 (30, 32) rows with flap measuring approx 2½ (2¾, 3)" [6.5 (7, 7.5)cm]. **Note:** For longer heel flap, work more rows, ending with a WS row; when working the gusset, pick up 1 st in each additional slipped st along edge of flap and dec until you reach original st count.

V-Heel Turn

Small and large only

Row 1 (RS): [K1, sl 1] 6 (7) times, ssk, k1, turn.

Row 2 (WS): Sl 1, p2, p2tog, p1, turn.

Row 3: [Sl 1, k1] twice, ssk, k1, turn.

Row 4: Sl 1, p4, p2tog, p1, turn.

Row 5: Sl 2, [k1, sl 1] twice, ssk, k1, turn.

Row 6: Sl 1, p6, p2tog, p1, turn.

Row 7: [Sl 1, k1] 4 times, ssk, k1, turn.

Row 8: Sl 1, p8, p2tog, p1, turn.

Row 9: Sl 2, [k1, sl 1] 4 times, ssk, k1, turn.

Row 10: Sl 1, p10, p2tog, p1, turn—13 sts. (end of size small)

Row 11: [Sl 1, k1] 6 times, ssk, k1, turn.

Row 12: Sl 1, p12, p2tog, p1, turn—15 sts. (end of size large)

Medium only

Row 1 (RS): [K1, sl 1] 6 times, k1, ssk, k1, turn.

Row 2 (WS): Sl 1, p2, p2tog, p1, turn.

Row 3: Sl 2, k1, sl 1, ssk, k1, turn.

Row 4: Sl 1, p4, p2tog, p1, turn.

Row 5: [Sl 1, k1] 3 times, ssk, k1, turn.

Row 6: Sl 1, p6, p2tog, p1, turn.

Row 7: Sl 2 [k1, sl 1] 3 times, ssk, k1, turn.

Row 8: Sl 1, p8, p2tog, p1, turn.

Row 9: [Sl 1, k1] 5 times, ssk, k1, turn.

Row 10: Sl 1, p10, p2tog, p1, turn.

Row 11: Sl 2 [k1, sl 1] 5 times, ssk, turn.

Row 12: Sl 1, p11, p2tog, turn—13 sts.

Gusset

Pick-up rnd: *N1:* Knit across heel sts, and with the same needle, pick up and knit 14 (15, 16) sts along side of heel flap, then M1 in the "corner" between heel flap and instep; *N2:* k21 (23, 25) instep sts; *N3:* M1 in "corner" working it tbl, then pick up and knit 14 (15, 16) sts along other side of heel flap, k6 (6, 7) heel sts from N1; mark beg of rnd—64 (68, 74) sts.

Rnd 1: Knit.

Rnd 2 (dec): *N1:* Knit to last 3 sts, ssk, k1; *N2:* knit; *N3:* k1, k2tog, knit to end of rnd—62 (66, 72) sts.

Rep [Rnds 1 and 2] 9 (9, 10) times—44 (48, 52) sts.

Foot

Work even in St st until foot measures approx 7¾ (8, 8½)" [19.5 (20.5, 21.5)cm] from back of heel with sock folded flat. **Note:** If your feet are shorter/longer, work even until foot measures approx *2½" [5.5cm] short of desired length.*

Toe

Rnd 1: Dec 2 (0, 4) sts evenly around—42 (48, 48) sts.

Rnd 2: *K1, sl 1; rep from * around.

Rnd 3: Knit.

Rnd 4: Rep rnd 2.

Rnd 5: *K5 (6, 6), ssk; rep from * around—36 (42, 42) sts.

Small only

Rnd 6: *[K1, sl 1] 3 times, [sl 1, k1] 3 times; rep from * around.

Rnd 7: Knit.

Rnd 8: Rep Rnd 6.

Medium and large only

Rnd 6: *[K1, sl 1] 3 times, k1; rep from * around.

Rnd 7: Knit.

Rnd 8: Rep rnd 6.

All sizes

Rnd 9: *K4 (5, 5), ssk; rep from * around—30 (36, 36) sts.

Rnd 10: *K1, sl 1; rep from * around.

Rnd 11: Knit.

Rnd 12: Rep rnd 10.

Rnd 13: *K3 (4, 4) sts, ssk; rep from * around—24 (30, 30) sts.

Small only

Rnd 14: *K2, ssk; rep from * around—18 sts.

Rnd 15: *K1, ssk; rep from * around—12 sts.

Rnd 16: Ssk around—6 sts.

Medium and large only

Rnd 14: *[K1, sl 1] twice, k1; rep from * around.

Rnd 15: Knit.

Rnd 16: Rep rnd 14.

Rnd 17: *K3, ssk; rep from * around—24 sts.

Rnd 18: *K2, ssk; rep from * around—18 sts.

Rnd 19: *K1, ssk; rep from * around—12 sts.

Rnd 20: Ssk around—6 sts.

Break yarn, leaving a 6" [15cm] tail. Using tapestry needle, thread tail through rem sts, and pull tight. Weave in all ends.

Block.

COLOR PATTERN

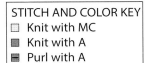

STITCH AND COLOR KEY
- ☐ Knit with MC
- ▨ Knit with A
- ▤ Purl with A
- ▨ Knit with B
- ▤ Purl with B
- ☐ Knit with C
- ▨ Knit with D
- ▤ Purl with D

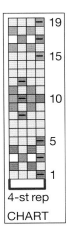

19

15

10

5

1

4-st rep

CHART

Uppsala Socks

Design by Chrissy Gardiner

Inspired by the wonderful textured colorwork of the Swedish Bohus knitting cooperative, founded by Emma Jacobsson in 1939, these fun, colorful socks integrate purl stitches into the colorwork design for added depth. Traditionally, Bohus designs were knit at nine stitches to the inch on 2.5 mm needles, sometimes including as many as 13 different colors per pattern.

Size
Women's medium [US sizes 6–8]

Finished Measurements
Length from cuff to ankle: 4½" [11.5cm]

Foot circumference: 7½" [19cm]

Materials 🧶**1**🧶
Alpaca with a Twist *Socrates* (fingering weight; 30% baby alpaca/30% merino wool/20% bamboo/20% nylon; 400yds [366m] per 3½ oz [100g] ball): 1 ball each Solar Explosion #5016 (MC), Jennifer's Yellow #5017 (A), and Natural #0100 (B)

Size 1 [2.25mm] double-pointed needles (set of 5) or size needed to obtain gauge

Stitch marker

Tapestry needle

Gauge
36 sts and 44 rnds = 4" [10cm] in St st.

Adjust needle size as necessary to obtain correct gauge.

Pattern Notes
This sock is worked from the cuff down with a square heel, gusset, and wedge toe.

This pattern can be worked using double-pointed needles, two circular needles, or on one long circular needle (using the Magic Loop method). To make the pattern more "universal," needles are not numbered, but stitches are instead referred to as "heel" and "instep." The heel (back of leg/sole) stitches are worked on the first two double-pointed needles or the first circular needle. The instep (front of leg/top of foot) stitches are worked on the last two double-pointed needles or the second circular needle.

Carry stranded yarn loosely to maintain elasticity of sock.

Weave in yarn not in use when carrying it more than 3 sts to avoid long floats inside socks.

Pattern Stitch
See Chart.

Instructions

Cuff

With A, CO 72 sts.

Arrange sts as follows: Place 18 sts on first dpn and 17 sts on second dpn (or 35 sts on first circular needle) for back of leg/heel; place 19 sts on third dpn and 18 sts on forth dpn (or 37 sts on second circular needle) for front of leg/instep. Mark beg of rnd and join, taking care not to twist sts.

Rnds 1–8: *K1 MC, p1 A; rep from * around. Break A.

Leg

Rnds 1–47: Work Rnds 1–17 of chart twice, then work Rnds 1–13 once more. Break B.

Heel Flap

Note: The heel flap is worked across the 35 heel sts. If working on dpns, transfer the 35 heel sts to a single dpn (the heel needle). Carry unused yarns on WS throughout heel flap and heel turn.

Row 1 (RS): Sl 1, [k1 MC, p1 A] 16 times, k2 MC.

Row 2: Sl 1, [p1 MC, k1 A] 16 times, p2 MC.

Rep [Rows 1 and 2] 11 more times.

Turn Heel

Row 1 (RS): Sl 1, [k1 MC, k1 A] 11 times, ssk MC, turn.

Row 2: Sl 1, [p1 A, p1 MC] 5 times, p1 A, p2tog MC, turn.

Row 3: S1 1, [k1 A, k1 MC] 5 times, k1 A, ssk MC, turn.

Row 4: Rep Row 2.

Rep Rows 3 and 4 until all side sts have been worked, ending with a WS row—13 heel sts. Break A.

Gusset

Pick-up and set-up rnds: Heel/sole sts: with RS facing and working with MC only, knit across 13 heel sts; with same needle, pick up and knit 13 sts along the left edge of heel flap (pick up 1 st in each sl-st chain along edge of heel flap and 1 st in join between heel and instep needles); instep sts: p1, *k1, p1; rep from * across 37 instep sts; heel/sole sts: with empty needle, pick up and knit 13 sts down right edge of heel flap as before, then k7 sts from second needle so that heel/sole sts are divided evenly over the two heel needles; knit to end of heel sts; work 37 instep sts in est rib—76 sts with beg of rnd between 37 instep and 39 heel/sole sts.

Rnd 1: Heel/sole: knit to last 3 sts, k2tog, k1; instep: work in est rib—75 sts.

Rnd 2: Heel/sole: k1, ssk, knit to end of heel sts; instep: work in est rib—74 sts.

Rep [Rnds 1 and 2] once more—72 sts.

Foot

Work sole sts in St st and instep sts in est rib until foot measures 3" [7.5cm] short of desired length.

Next 12 rnds: Work Rnds 1–12 of chart. Break B.

Next rnd: With MC, knit across sole sts; k1, ssk, knit to last 3 instep sts, k2tog, k1—70 sts.

Toe

Rnd 1: *[K1 MC, k1 A] to last sole st, k1 MC; rep from * across instep sts.

Rnd 2 (dec): *K1 MC, ssk A, [k1 A, k1 MC] to last 4 sole sts, k1 A, k2tog A, k1 MC; rep from * across instep sts—66 sts.

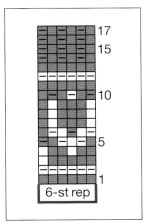

Rnd 3: *K1 MC, k2 A, [k1 MC, k1 A] to last 2 sole sts, k1 A, k1 MC; rep from * across instep sts.

Rnd 4 (dec): *K1 MC, ssk A, [k1 MC, k1 A] to last 4 sole sts, k1 MC, k2tog A, k1; rep from * across instep sts—62 sts.

Cont working in this manner, maintaining stripe pat with 1 st MC at each end of instep and sole and working decs with A; work decs every other rnd until 38 sts rem, then work decs every rnd until 22 sts rem (11 sts each instep and sole).

Finishing

Break yarns, leaving MC tail of 14–18" [35-45cm].

With tapestry needle and MC tail, graft toe closed using Kitchener st.

Weave in all ends. Block.

COLOR PATTERN

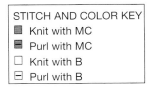

STITCH AND COLOR KEY
- Knit with MC
- Purl with MC
- Knit with B
- Purl with B

Norwegian Socks

Design by Kristin Spurkland

Inspired by memories of childhood hikes in the forests and on the fjords in Norway (and the hand-knit socks my relatives wore on those hikes), these socks utilize traditional Norwegian patterns and colors. The design features a Selbu Star, a popular motif in the Norwegian knitting tradition. Although the patterning is complex, the gusset panels on the calves and the herringbone pattern down the back of the leg allow for achieving a customized fit without much trouble.

Size
Women's medium [US sizes 8–9]

Finished Measurements
Foot circumference: 8" [20.5cm]

Calf circumference: 14½" [37cm]

Foot length: 9" [23cm]

Materials 🧶**1**🧶
ShibuiKnits *Sock* (fingering weight; 100% superwash merino; 191yds [175m] per 1¾ oz [50g] skein): 3 skeins Midnight (A), two skeins Ivory (B)

Size 1 [2.25mm] double-pointed needles (set of 5)

Size 3 [3.25mm] double-pointed needles (set of 5) or size needed to obtain gauge

Stitch markers

Tapestry needle

Gauge
32 sts and 32 rnds = 4" [10cm] in stranded St st.

Adjust needle size as necessary to obtain correct gauge.

Pattern Notes
This sock is worked from the cuff down, with a shaped calf gusset, a flap heel, and a wedge toe.

Variations in fit can be achieved by adjusting needle size up or down. For thinner calves, ribbing may be worked on smaller needle; for thicker calves, work ribbing on larger needle.

The calf can also be adjusted by adding or subtracting sts in the calf-gusset panels.

For smaller socks, the main pattern can be knit on smaller needles.

For the best results, try on the sock several times while knitting, to ensure the desired fit is being achieved, and adjust needle size/stitch count as necessary.

Strand the yarn not in use loosely on WS to maintain elasticity of fabric; do not carry yarn not in use more than 5 sts—weave it in as necessary.

Instructions

Cuff

With smaller needles and A, CO 84 sts. Distribute sts evenly on 4 dpns; mark beg of rnd and join, taking care not to twist sts.

Work in K2, P2 Rib for 4" [10cm].

Next rnd: Change to larger dpns; knit and inc 20 sts evenly around—104 sts.

Leg

Set-up rnd: Work Calf Chart over first 39 sts; k7 A for gusset panel and mark center st; k1 B, work Main Pattern Chart over next 49 sts, k1 B; k7 A for gusset panel and mark center st.

Rnds 2-6: Work pats and colors as est.

Shape Calf

Gusset Inc Rnd: *Work est pats to marked center st of gusset panel, M1, k1, M1; rep from * once, work to end—108 sts.

Maintaining est pats, rep Gusset Inc Rnd [every 5th rnd] twice, working new sts with A—116 sts.

Work even until Rnd 6 of 2nd rep of Main pat is complete.

Gusset Dec Rnd: *Work to 1 st before marked center st of gusset panel, S2K2P; rep from * once, work to end—112 sts.

Maintaining est pat, rep Gusset Dec Rnd [every 3rd rnd] 6 times, and on the last Gusset Dec Rnd, work the dec with B—88 sts with all gusset sts eliminated and 1 st B each side between Calf pat and Main pat.

Work even until Rnd 3 of third rep of Main pat is complete.

Calf Dec Rnd: Work to 1 st before center st of Calf Panel, S2KP2 with B, work to end of rnd—86 sts.

Maintaining est pat, rep Calf Dec Rnd [every 3rd rnd] 11 times— 64 sts.

Work even until 4 reps of Main pat are complete. Break both yarns.

Heel Flap

Set up: Slip first 23 sts of rnd onto 1 dpn for heel; place next 33 sts onto 2 dpns for instep; slip last 8 sts to heel dpn—31 heel sts on 1 dpn.

Row 1 (WS): With the WS facing, join A and purl a row.

Row 2 (RS): *Sl 1, k1; rep from * to last st, k1.

Row 3: Sl 1, purl to end.

Rep [Rows 2 and 3] 15 times.

Turn Heel

Row 1 (RS): K18, k2tog, k1, turn.

Row 2: Sl 1, p6, p2tog, p1.

Row 3: Sl 1, k7, ssk, k1.

Row 4: Sl 1, p8, p2tog, p1.

Row 5: Sl 1, k8, ssk, k1.

Row 6: Sl 1, p10, p2tog, p1.

Cont in this manner until all the heel sts have been worked—19 heel sts rem.

Break yarn.

Heel Gusset

Pick-up rnd: With spare dpn (N1) and A, and beg at point where right-hand side of flap (as you are looking at it) meets instep sts, pick up and knit 10 st along flap, then with A and B, pick up 6 sts following Sole Chart; knit 8 heel sts continuing Sole Chart; with another dpn (N2), knit rem 9 heel sts following Sole Chart, then pick up and knit 6 sts along left side of flap, ending Sole Chart; with A, pick up 10 sts to end of flap; N3 and N4: work 33 instep sts following Instep Chart—84 sts with 10 gusset sts each side and 31 sole sts on N1 and N2 and 33 instep sts on N3 and N4.

Rnd 1: N1: Ssk, work in est pats to end; N2: work in est pats to last 2 sts, k2tog; N3 and N4: work est Instep pat—82 sts.

Rnd 2: Work even in est pats.

Rep [Rnds 1 and 2] 8 times—66 sts.

Next rnd: N1: K2tog with B, work to end; N2: work to last 2 sts, ssk with B; N3 and N4: work est Instep pat—64 sts with 31 sole sts and 33 instep sts.

Foot

Work even in est pats until Instep Chart has been worked twice, or until foot is approximately 2½" [6.5cm] short of desired length.

Break B.

Toe

Rnd 1: Knit with A only.

Rnd 2: N1 and N2: knit; N3: k1, ssk, knit to end; N4: knit to last 3 sts, k2tog, k1—62 sts.

Rnd 3: *N1: k1, ssk, knit to end; N2: knit to last 3 sts, k2tog, k1; N3 and N4: rep from *—58 sts.

Rep [Rnd 3] 9 times—22 sts.

Finishing

Break yarn, leaving a 12" [30.5cm] tail. Transfer sts on N2 to N1 and sts on N4 to N3—11 sts on each needle. With tapestry needle and tail, graft toe closed using Kitchener st. Weave in ends. Block sock.

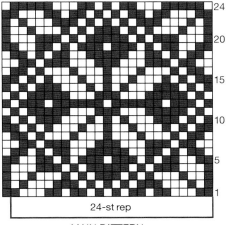

MAIN PATTERN

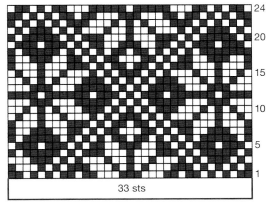

INSTEP CHART

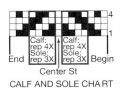

CALF AND SOLE CHART

COLOR KEY
- ■ A
- □ B

Gansey Socks

Design by Beth Brown-Reinsel

These Gansey Socks were inspired by the wonderful fisherman sweaters created in Britain in the nineteenth century. The construction includes a back seam made of a baby cable, starfish, and panels with diagonal lines; a slip-stitch heel; a square (German) heel turning; wedge-toe shaping; and Kitchener stitch for finishing the toes. The socks feature the classic Channel Island Cast-On. This decorative and substantial cast-on forms a strand of "beads" along the beginning edge of the garment that accentuates, by contrast, the horizontal lines of a garter welt.

Size
Women's medium [US sizes 8–9]

Finished Measurements
Length from cuff to ankle: 6½" [16.5cm]

Length from cuff to heel: 9⅜" [24 cm]

Foot circumference: 8" [20.5cm]

Materials 🧶2
Frangipani *5-ply Guernsey Wool* (sport weight; 100% wool; 1,200yds [1,097m] per 17¾ oz [500g] cone): approx 300yds [274m]. Shown in Amethyst. You can substitute any sport-weight wool yarn for a firm, warm sock, or a fingering-weight sock yarn for a lighter sock.

Size 2 [2.75mm] double-pointed needles (set of 4) or size needed to obtain gauge

Tapestry needle

Gauge
28 sts and 40 rnds = 4" [10cm] in St st.

Adjust needle size as necessary to obtain correct gauge.

Pattern Notes
This sock is worked with 4 double-point needles from the cuff down with a heel flap, German/square heel turn, and a wedge toe.

The needles are identified as N1, N2, and N3 in the order that they are used. After the leg is worked, the heel flap stitches (centered above the back mini-cable seam) are put on N3, with the instep stitches remaining on hold on N1 and N2. When working the foot, N1 and N3 hold the heel/gusset/sole sts and N2 holds the instep sts.

Special Abbreviations
Tw2R (Twist 2 Right): K2tog but do not remove from LH needle. Knit into the first st again and take both sts off left needle.

N1, N2, N3: Needle 1, needle 2, needle 3

Special Technique

The Channel Island Cast-On

This technique forms two stitches at once. Two strands of yarn are used together to wind around the thumb forming the bead, while a third strand is used to form the stitches. You can use both ends of one skein plus one end from a piece broken off from your ball (about 60" [152cm] long).

Holding three yarns together as one, make a slip knot 6" [15cm] from the end.

The slip knot itself is made of three loops, being formed from three strands of yarn held as one. When working this method, do not count the slip knot—you can remove and pull out that first stitch after the first round has been worked without harm to the rest of your stitches.

1. *Hold the single yarn over your left forefinger and wrap the other two yarns twice around your left thumb in a counter-clockwise direction. Your needle is in your right hand.

2. Bring the needle over, behind, and under the single yarn, just like a yarn over. (This forms the first of the two stitches made.)

3. Then insert your needle up into the two loops on the thumb (this forms the bead).

4. Pick up the single yarn again as for Step 3 (this is the second stitch), pull the new stitch through the thumb loops, tension the stitch, and rep from *.

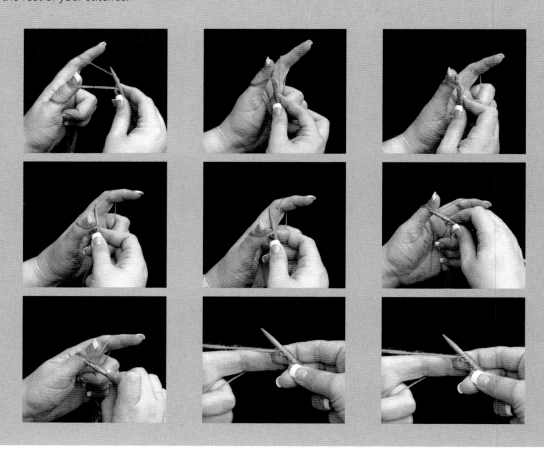

Stitch Pattern

A chart is provided for those who prefer working from charts.

Rnd 1: P1, k2, p1, k2, [p1, k1] 3 times, k7, [p1, k1] 3 times, k16, [p1, k1] 3 times, k7, [p1, k1] 3 times, k1.

Rnd 2: P1, k2, p1, k8, p1, k39, p1, k8.

Rnd 3: P1, Tw2R, p1, k2, [p1, k1] 3 times, p2, k5, [p1, k1] 3 times, k4, p1, k5, p1, k5, [p1, k1] 3 times, k4, p2, k1, [p1, k1] 3 times, k1.

Rnd 4: P1, k2, p1, k9, p2, k14, p2, k3, p2, k14, p2, k9.

Rnd 5: P1, k2, p1, k2, [p1, k1] 3 times, k2, p2, k3, [p1, k1] 3 times, k4, p3, k1, p3, k5, [p1, k1] 3 times, k2, p2, k3, [p1, k1] 3 times, k1.

Rnd 6: P1, k2, p1, k11, p2, k13, p2, k1, p2, k13, p2, k11.

Rnd 7: P1, Tw2R, p1, k2, [p1, k1] 3 times, k4, p2, k1 [p1, k1] 3 times, k6, p1, k1, p1, k7, [p1, k1] 3 times, p2, k5, [p1, k1] 3 times, k1.

Rnd 8: P1, k2, p1, k13, p1, k8, p3, k7, p3, k8, p1, k13.

Rnd 9: P1, k2, p1, k2, [p1, k1] 3 times, k7, [p1, k1] 3 times, k2, p3, k5, p3, k3, [p1, k1] 3 times, k7, [p1, k1] 3 times, k1.

Rnd 10: P1, k2, p1, k24, p3, k3, p3, k24.

Rnd 11: P1, Tw2R, p1, k2, [p1, k1] 3 times, k7, [p1, k1] 3 times, k4, p3, k1, p3, k5 [p1, k1] 3 times, k7, [p1. k1] 3 times, k1.

Rnd 12: P1, k2, p1, k8, p1, k15, p3, k3, p3, k15, p1, k8.

Rnd 13: P1, k2, p1, k2, [p1, k1] 3 times, p2, k5, [p1, k1] 3 times, k2, p3, k5, p3, k3, [p1, k1] 3 times, k4, p2, k1, [p1, k1] 3 times, k1.

Rnd 14: P1, k2, p1, k9, p2, k11, p3, k7, p3, k11, p2, p9.

Rnd 15: P1, Tw2R, p1, k2, [p1, k1] 3 times, k2, p2, k3, [p1, k1] 3 times, k6, p1, k1, p1, k7, [p1, k1] 3 times, k2, p2, k3, [p1, k1] 3 times, k1.

Rnd 16: P1, k2, p1, k11, p2, k13, p2, k1, p2, k13, p2, k11.

Rnd 17: P1, k2, p1, k2, [p1, k1] 3 times, k4, p2, k1, [p1, k1] 3 times, k4, p3, k1, p3, k5, [p1, k1] 3 times, p2, k5, [p1, k1] 3 times, k1.

Rnd 18: P1, k2, p1, k13, p1, k11, p2, k3, p2, k11, p1, k13.

Rnd 19: P1, Tw2R, p1, k2, [p1, k1] 3 times, k7, [p1, k1] 3times, k4, p1, k5, p1, k5, [p1, k1] 3 times, k7, [p1, k1] 3 times, k1.

Rnd 20: P1, k2, p1, knit to end of rnd.

Rep Rnds 1-20 for pat.

Instructions

Using the Channel Island method, cast on 54 sts, dividing sts evenly among 3 dpns: 18-18-18. Remove slipknot and join, being careful not to twist.

Garter Welt

Rnd 1: Knit, increasing 7 sts evenly around—61 sts divided 20-21-20.

Rnds 2 and 4: Purl.

Rnd 3: Knit.

Leg

Work 20-rnd pat 3 times—60 rnds.

Rearrange Sts for Heel Flap And Instep Sts

With N3, work 18 sts from N1 (2 sts left on N1); sl 13 sts from N2 to N1; sl 6 sts from N3 to N2—sts now arranged 15-14-32. The 32 sts on N3 are heel sts; the rem 29 sts will be held for the instep.

Heel Flap

Turn your work so that the WS of the heel is facing you; work heel sts back and forth in rows.

Row 1 (WS): Sl 1 pwise wyif, purl to end.

Row 2 (RS): *Sl 1 pwise wyib, k1, rep from * to end.

Rep [Rows 1 and 2] 13 times—28 rows.

Purl 1 row.

Heel Turn

Row 1 (RS): K20, ssk, turn.

Row 2: Sl 1 pwise, p8, p2tog, turn.

Row 3: Sl 1 pwise, k8, ssk, turn.

Rep Rows 2 and 3 until 10 sts rem ready to work a RS row.

Gusset

Slip 29 instep sts to 1 dpn (now N2).

Rnd 1: N1: K10 heel sts, then pick up and knit 17 sts along the side of the heel flap; N2: beg with Row 1, work charted pat across 29 instep sts; N3: pick up and knit 17 sts down other side of heel flap, then k5 from N1—73 sts distributed as 22-29-22. The beg of rnd is now at center heel/sole.

Rnd 2: N1: K21, then slip last st to N2; N2: k2tog, work in est pat across 27 sts, work an ssk with the last st of N2 and the first st of N3; N3: k21—71 sts. **Note:** This rnd eliminates the gap between the instep and heel sts.

Rnd 3: N1: Knit to last 3 sts, k2tog, k1; N2: work 29 sts of pat on instep; N3: k1, ssk, k18—69 sts.

Rnd 4: Work even in est pats (Gansey pat on instep sts, St st on sole sts).

Rep [Rnds 3 and 4] 4 times—61 sts distributed as 16-29-16.

Foot

Work even in est pats until 3 reps of instep pat are complete. **Note:** Three reps yields a sock which will fit a woman wearing a US size 8–9 shoe. To adjust for length, knit all rounds after the 3rd rep until foot measures 2½" [6.5cm] shorter than desired length.

Toe

Rnd 1: N1: K2tog, knit to last 3 sts, k2tog, k1; N2: knit; N3: k1, ssk, knit to end—58 sts distributed as 14-29-15.

Rnd 2: Knit.

Rnd 3: N1: Knit to last 3 sts, k2tog, k1; N2: k1, ssk, knit to last 3 sts, k2tog, k1; N3: k1, ssk, knit to end—54 sts.

Rep [Rnds 2 and 3] 9 times, then with N3, knit to end of N1—18 sts distributed 9-9.

Break yarn leaving a 12" [30.5cm] tail.

With tapestry needle and tail, graft toe closed using Kitchener st.

Finishing

Weave in all ends.

Block with steam iron.

Stitch Key	
□	Knit
⊟	Purl
⧄⧅	Tw2R

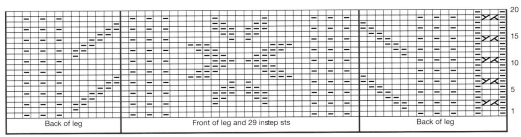

GANSEY PATTERN

Back of leg | Front of leg and 29 instep sts | Back of leg

Short-Row
Fair Isle Socks

Design by Teva Durham

Traditional Fair Isle knitting, a stranded technique in which no more than two colors are used in one row, originated on Fair Isle, one of the Shetland Islands located north of Scotland. In early Fair Isle knitting, any given color was not repeated for more than three stitches in a row to prevent long strands between colors on the back of the work. Here's a modern version of a Fair Isle sock with a twist: short rows are used to interrupt the predictable bands of color, shifting the pattern to create a diagonal band.

Size
Women's medium/large [US sizes 7–12]

Finished Measurements
Length from cuff to ankle: 8" [20.5cm]

Foot circumference: 9" [23cm]

Materials 🧶4🧶
Loop-d-Loop by Teva Durham *Moss* (DK weight; 85% extrafine merino wool/15% nylon; 163yds [149m] per 1¾ oz [50g] ball): 2 balls Fuchsia #07 (MC); 1 ball each Brown #02 (A), Light Lilac #05 (B), and Crimson #10 (C)

Size 2 [2.75mm] circular needle or size needed to obtain gauge

Size 2 [2.75mm] double-pointed needles (set of 5)

Size G/6 [4mm] crochet hook for trim

Stitch marker

Tapestry needle

Gauge
24 sts and 32 rows = 4" [10cm] in 2-color stranded St st.

Adjust needle size as necessary to obtain correct gauge.

Pattern Notes
The sock is worked from cuff to toe.

The leg is worked back and forth on a circular needle to allow for short-row patterning and for starting a row from either edge. Whenever necessary in pattern, cut yarn and slide stitches to opposite end of needle to start next row.

After the leg is complete, stitches from the beginning and end of the leg are joined for the heel flap and heel turn. The sock is worked in the round from the gusset to the toe.

The left and right socks have mirrored symmetry; the short rows are begun on opposite sides for each sock.

Carry stranded yarn loosely to maintain sock's elasticity.

Stitch Patterns

Stripe Pattern

*Work 1 row A, 2 rows MC; rep from *, ending 1 row A.

Color Patterns

See Charts.

Instructions

First Sock

Cuff

With circular needle and A, CO 61 sts.

Beg and end with a WS row, work 7 rows in K1, P1 Rib in the Stripe pat.

Leg

Rows 1–8: Begin St st and work Chart A.

Rows 9–15: Work Stripe pat.

Short-Row Patterning

Slide sts to other end of needle, ready to work a RS row.

Work decreasing short rows while working Chart A (**Note:** Chart A begins on a RS row for this series of short rows):

Short-row set 1: K39, W&T; purl to end.

Short-row set 2: K33 (6 sts before last wrap), W&T; purl to end.

Short-row set 3: K27 (6 sts before last wrap), W&T; purl to end.

Short-row set 4: K21 (6 sts before last wrap), W&T; purl to end.

Cut C.

Slide sts to other end of needle, ready to work a WS row.

Next row (WS): With A, purl across all sts with A, hiding all wraps.

Next 13 rows: Work Chart B across all sts. Cut MC.

Note: The short rows make this motif appear to be slanted.

Slide sts to other end of needle, ready to work a RS row.

Next row (RS): Knit with A.

Work increasing short rows while working Chart A (**Note:** Chart A begins on a WS row for this series of short rows):

Short-row set 1: P22, W&T; k22.

Short-row set 2: P28 sts (5 sts past wrapped st—hide the wrap as you pass it), W&T; k28.

Short-row set 3: P34 (5 sts past previous wrap (hiding wrap), W&T; k34.

Short-row set 4: P40 (5 sts past previous wrap (hiding wrap), W&T; k40.

Shape Ankle

Rows 1–7: Beg and end with a WS row, work Stripe pat and *at the same time*, dec 1 st at each end on Row 4 as follows: K1, k2tog, knit to last 3 sts, ssk, k1—59 sts.

Row 8 (RS): K1 B, k2tog with B, k2 B, work Row 1 of Chart A to last 3 sts, ssk with B, k1 B—57 sts.

Rows 9–15: Cont working Chart A as est, and on pat Row 5, dec at each end once more—55 sts. Cut B and C.

Row 16: With A, knit across.

Heel Flap

With RS facing, slip first and last 14 sts to 1 dpn for heel flap, leaving rem 27 sts on hold on circular needle for instep.

Row 1 (WS): With another dpn and MC, purl across 28 heel sts.

Cont in St st and Stripe pat as est; work even until flap measures 2½" [6.5cm], ending with a WS row.

Cut A and cont with MC only.

Turn Heel

Row 1 (RS): K17, ssk, k1, turn.

Row 2 (WS): Sl 1, p7, p2tog, p1, turn.

Row 3: Sl 1, k8, ssk, k1, turn.

Row 4: Sl 1, p9, p2tog, p1, turn.

Cont working in this manner, working 1 more st on each row until all sts have been worked, ending with a WS row—18 sts.

Gusset

Pick-up rnd: N1: K18 heel sts, then pick up and knit 14 sts along the left edge of flap; N2 and N3: knit across 27 instep sts; N4: pick up and knit 14 sts along right edge of flap, k9 heel sts from N1; mark beg of rnd—73 sts with 23 sts on N1, 27 instep sts on N2 and N3 combined, and 23 sts on N4.

Rnd 1: N1: Knit to last 3 sts, k2tog, k1; N2 and N3: knit; N4: k1, ssk, knit to end—71 sts.

Rnd 2: Knit.

Rep [Rnds 1 and 2] 8 more times—55 sts with 14 sts on N1, 27 sts on N2 and N3 combined, 14 sts on N4.

Foot

Work even in est pats until foot measures approx 8" [20.5cm] from back of heel or 2" [5cm] short of desired length.

Toe

Rnd 1 (dec): N1: Knit to last 3 sts, k2tog, k1; N2: ssk, knit to end; N3: knit to last 2 sts, k2tog; N4: k1, ssk, work to end—53 sts.

Rnd 2: Knit around.

Rep [Rnds 1 and 2] 5 times, then [Rnd 1] 4 times—17 sts.

With N4, work across N1 as follows: knit to last 3 sts, k2tog, k1; transfer sts from N2 to N3—16 sts with 8 sts on each dpn.

Break yarn, leaving a 12" [30.5cm] tail.

With tapestry needle and tail, graft toe closed using Kitchener st.

Finishing

Weave in all ends.

Block.

Sew back leg seam (the pattern will not match across short-row section).

Trim

With crochet hook and 1 strand each MC and A held together, work trim down back leg seam as follows: place slipknot on hook, ch 1, hold yarn to front of work, *insert hook through st at top of cuff, pull up a loop, ch 1; rep from *, working down to heel. Cut yarn and pull through last loop to secure. Pull ends to WS of sock and weave in.

Second Sock

Work as for first sock, but reverse the short rows to create a mirror image as follows: begin first series of decreasing short rows on a WS (purl) row; begin second series of increasing short rows on a RS (knit) row.

COLOR KEY
- ■ MC
- □ B
- ■ C

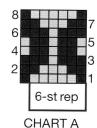

6-st rep

CHART A

Note: For some short rows RS and WS rows may be reversed, i.e., Row 1 may be a WS row.

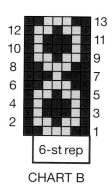

6-st rep

CHART B

SOCKS

He' Mo Leannan
Kilt Hose

Design by Anne Carroll Gilmour

He' mo Leannan is the name of a favorite *orain luadh* (waulking song) that means: "Hey my Love!" in Gaelic, and it was one of the first waulking songs I ever learned to sing in this beautiful language. I designed these kilt hose for my husband, adapting the knot on our wedding bands for the cuffs and central motif, so I thought the title of this song would be an appropriate name for the pattern.

Sizes
Men's medium [US sizes 10½–13] (large [US sizes 14–15]). Instructions are given for smaller size, with larger size in parentheses. When only 1 number is given, it applies to both sizes.

Finished Measurements
Cuff-to-flap length: 13 (14½)" [33 (37)cm]

Calf circumference: 12 (13½)" [30.5 (34.5)cm]

Foot circumference: 9½ (11)" [24 (28)cm]

Materials 🧶1 or 🧶3
Wendy *Guernsey 5-ply* (fingering weight; 100% wool; 245yds [224m] per 3½ oz [100g] ball): 3 (4) balls Natural #500

Froehlich Wolle *Sedrun* (DK weight; 90% wool/10% nylon; 131yds [120m] per 1¾ oz [50g] ball): 6 balls Dark Green #5566

Size 1 (2) [2.25 (2.75)mm)] double-pointed needles (set of 4)

Size 2 (3) [2.75 (3.25)mm] double-pointed needles (set of 4) or size needed to obtain gauge

Size D/3 [3.25mm] crochet hook

6 stitch markers, 1 in CC for beg of rnd

Tapestry needle

Gauge
26 (24) sts and 32 (30) rnds = 4" (10cm) in St st with fingering (DK) yarn and size 2 (3) needles.

Adjust needle size as necessary to obtain correct gauge.

Pattern Notes
This sock is worked from cuff to toe. The cuff border is worked flat, then grafted into a ring; picot hems/edges are worked on both sides of the turned-down cuff, after which the sock is worked to the toe, with the leg shaped with a calf gusset, heel flap and heel gusset, and wedge toe.

The sample socks worked in the green DK-weight yarn used the medium instructions; the sample socks worked with the cream hard-spun Guernsey yarn used the large instructions. You can vary the sizes by working the medium size with Guernsey yarn or the large size with DK yarn. For women's sizes, use a fingering-weight sock yarn with a denser gauge than the Guernsey yarn and follow medium instructions.

This pattern gives you multiple pattern options for back leg cables and side "knit/purl" panels. You never have to knit the same pair twice!

Instructions

Cuff

Cuff Border

Using provisional method and larger dpn, CO 15 sts.

With larger dpns and working back and forth, work 4 reps of Cuff Chart.

Unzip waste yarn of provisional CO; graft live sts to live CO sts to form a ring.

Turned Picot Hem

Bottom of cuff when it's turned down

With larger dpns, pick up (but don't knit) under all the purl bumps around the ring; mark beg of rnd—56 (60) sts on dpns.

Rnd 1: Knit and inc 12 (16) sts evenly around—68 (76) sts.

Rnds 2–5: Work in garter st (knit 1 rnd, purl 1 rnd).

Rnds 6–8: Knit.

Rnd 9 (picot turning rnd): [Yo, k2tog] around.

Rnds 10–12 (hem): Knit.

Bind-off rnd: Turn the hem edge up behind your cuff with purl sides together (it will fold nicely along the line of picot stitches); carefully catch the first hem st with its corresponding cuff st and knit these 2 sts tog; *knit the next hem st tog with the next cuff st; BO 1 st very loosely; rep from * around. **Notes:** Try not to pull your working yarn too tightly while binding off to maintain elasticity of cuff. Make sure you continue working stitch for stitch—if you off-set any of the sts your hem will twist in an unattractive manner.

Turned Picot Cuff Top

Work 12 rnds as for Turned Picot Hem.

Joining rnd: Turn the edge up behind your cuff with purl sides together as before; carefully catch the first live st with its corresponding cuff st and knit these 2 sts tog; *knit the next live st tog with the next cuff st; rep from * around. *Do not bind off*—68 (76) sts rem.

Ribbed Garter

Switch to smaller dpns.

Work 23 rnds in K2, P2 Rib for sock "garter."

Reverse Cuff

With yarn at back, slip first st to the RH needle. Bring yarn forward and transfer st back to LH needle, then turn the work as if you were knitting flat. Flip the entire cuff inside out through the ring formed by your dpns so that you can work in the opposite direction—you have, in effect, made a wrapped st "U-turn," so that when the cuff is folded down as worn, the RS of the work will show.

Leg

Leg has 6 panels around: Calf Chart, Back Leg Cable of choice, K/P pat A of choice, Center Knot pat, K/P pat B of choice, Back Leg Cable of choice. 1 st is slipped between each panel every other rnd.

Set-up rnd: Switch to larger dpns; sl 1, p19, sl 1, pm; p1 (2), [k1, M1] 4 times, k1, M1p, p0 (1), pm; sl 1, p1 (2), k6, p1 (2), pm; work Rnd 1 of Center Front Knot Chart over the next 17 sts (center front leg), pm; p1 (2), k6, p1 (2), sl 1, pm; p1 (2), [k1, M1] 4 times, k1, M1p, p0 (1); mark beg of rnd—78 (86) sts. **Note:** This rnd counts as Rnd 1 of all leg pattern charts.

Rnd 2: Working Rnd 2 of each chart, work Calf Chart over 21 sts to first marker, sm; work Back Leg Cable Chart of choice over 11 (13) sts, sm; work K/P Chart A of choice over 9 (11) sts, sm; work Center Knot Chart over 17 sts, sm; work K/P Chart B of choice over 9 (11) sts, sm; work Back Leg Cable Chart of your choice over 11 (13) sts.

Work in est pats until Calf Chart is complete—1 st rem for Calf. On following rnds, work that st as: sl 1 on odd rnds and k1-tbl on even rnds—62 (70) sts.

Cont in est pats until Center Knot Chart is complete, then work even, purling all sts between slipped sts of Center Knot Panel, until sock reaches desired length to heel flap—54 (62) sts.

Divide for Heel Flap

Change to smaller dpns for remainder of sock.

With smaller dpn, k14 (16) sts; keep 27 (31) center front sts on hold for instep; transfer rem 13 (15) back leg sts to first dpn for heel flap—27 (31) heel flap sts.

Heel Flap

Row 1 (WS): K1, yf, *sl 1, p1; rep from * to last 2 sts, sl 1; yb, k1.

Row 2 (RS): Knit across.

Rep [Rows 1 and 2] 12 (13) times—26 (28) rows.

Turn Heel

Row 1 (WS): K1, yf, [sl 1, p1] 7 (8) times, p2tog, p1; turn. 9, 11

Row 2 (RS): Sl 1, k4, ssk, k1; turn.

Row 3: [Sl 1, p1] 3 times, p2tog, p1; turn. 7, 9

Row 4: Sl 1, k6, ssk, k1; turn.

Row 5: Sl 1, p2, [sl 1, p1] twice, sl 1, p2tog, p1; turn. 5, 7

Row 6: Sl 1, k8, ssk, k1; turn.

Row 7: [Sl 1, p1] 5 times, p2tog, p1; turn. 3, 5

Row 8: Sl 1, k10, ssk, k1; turn.

Row 9: Sl 1, p2, [sl 1, p1] 4 times, sl 1, p2tog, p1; turn. 1, 3

Row 10: Sl 1, k12, ssk, k1, turn.

Row 11: [Sl 1, p1] 7 times, p2tog, p0 (1); turn.

Row 12: Sl 1, k13 (14), ssk, k0 (1); turn for large.

Medium heel is complete; do not turn—15 sts.

Large Only

Row 13: Sl 1, p2, [sl 1, p1] 6 times, sl 1, p2tog; turn.

Row 14: Sl 1, k15, ssk; do not turn—17 sts.

Heel Gusset

Note: When working K/P pat on instep, complete last pat rep from leg (if necessary), then work Rnd 1 only of chart to toe shaping.

Set-up rnd: N1: With dpn holding heel sts, pick up and knit into first 12 (13) garter bumps along side of heel flap, then pick up and *purl* into last bump; N2 (instep sts): work in est pat as follows: maintaining slip-st chains between panels, work K/P pat; p11 sts from Center Front Panel; work K/P pat; N3: pick up and purl into first garter bump of heel flap, then pick up and knit into rem 12 (13) bumps; k7 (8) heel sts from N1—68 (76) sts with 21 (23) sts on N1; 27 (31) sts on N2; and 20 (22) sts on N3.

Rnd 1 (dec): N1: Knit to last 3 sts, k2tog, p1; N2: work as est; N3: p1, ssk, knit to end—66 (74) sts.

Rnd 2: N1: Knit to last st, p1; N2: work as est; N3: p1, knit to end.

Rep [Rnds 1 and 2] 6 times—54 (62) sts.

Next rnd: N1: Knit to last 3 sts, k2tog, p1; N2 and N3: work as est—53 (61) sts with 13 (15) sts each on N1 and N3 and 27 (31) sts on N2.

Foot

Work even in est pats until foot measures approx 2 (2½)" [5 (6.5)cm] short of desired length.

Toe

Dec rnd: N1: Knit to last 3 sts, k2tog, k1; N2: k1, ssk, knit to last 3 sts, k2tog, k1; N3: ssk, knit to end—49 (57) sts.

Rnd 2: N1: *K1, sl 1; rep from * to last 3 sts, k3; N2: k2, *k1, sl 1; rep from * to last 3 sts, k3; N3: K2, *k1, sl 1; rep from * end.

Rep Dec rnd [every other rnd] 8 (10) times, maintaining est heel-st pat on even rnds.

Finishing

Break yarn, leaving a 18" [46cm] tail. With tapestry needle and tail, graft toe closed using Kitchener st. Wet block socks to finished measurements.

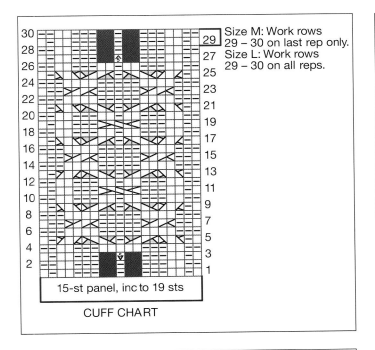

Size M: Work rows
29 – 30 on last rep only.
Size L: Work rows
29 – 30 on all reps.

15-st panel, inc to 19 sts

CUFF CHART

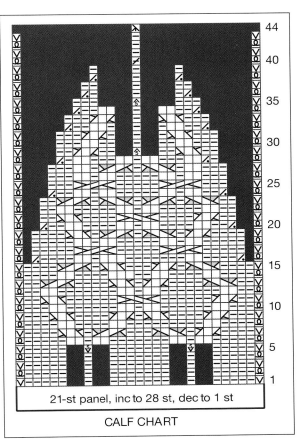

21-st panel, inc to 28 st, dec to 1 st

CALF CHART

STITCH KEY

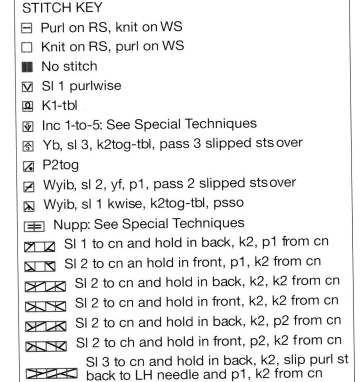

- ⊟ Purl on RS, knit on WS
- ☐ Knit on RS, purl on WS
- ■ No stitch
- ☑ Sl 1 purlwise
- Ⓞ K1-tbl
- ☑ Inc 1-to-5: See Special Techniques
- ☑ Yb, sl 3, k2tog-tbl, pass 3 slipped sts over
- ☑ P2tog
- ☑ Wyib, sl 2, yf, p1, pass 2 slipped sts over
- ☒ Wyib, sl 1 kwise, k2tog-tbl, psso
- ⊞ Nupp: See Special Techniques
- Sl 1 to cn and hold in back, k2, p1 from cn
- Sl 2 to cn an hold in front, p1, k2 from cn
- Sl 2 to cn and hold in back, k2, k2 from cn
- Sl 2 to cn and hold in front, k2, k2 from cn
- Sl 2 to cn and hold in back, k2, p2 from cn
- Sl 2 to ch and hold in front, p2, k2 from cn
- Sl 3 to cn and hold in back, k2, slip purl st back to LH needle and p1, k2 from cn
- Sl 3 to cn and hold in front, k2, slip purl st back to LH needle and p1, k2 from cn

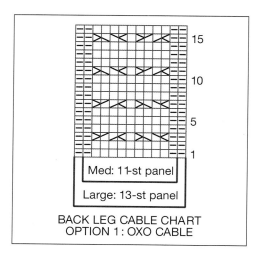

BACK LEG CABLE CHART
OPTION 1: OXO CABLE

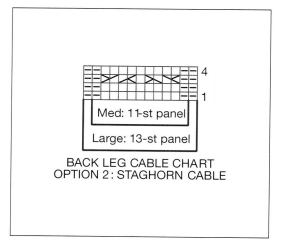

BACK LEG CABLE CHART
OPTION 2: STAGHORN CABLE

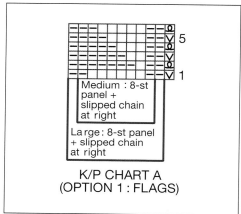

K/P CHART A
(OPTION 1 : FLAGS)

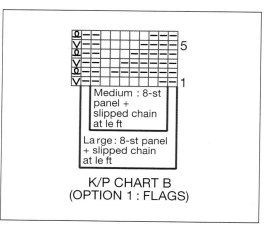

K/P CHART B
(OPTION 1 : FLAGS)

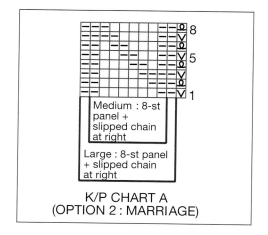

K/P CHART A
(OPTION 2 : MARRIAGE)

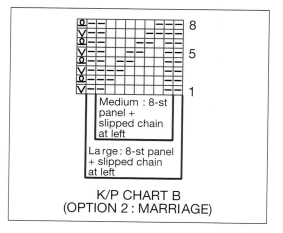

K/P CHART B
(OPTION 2 : MARRIAGE)

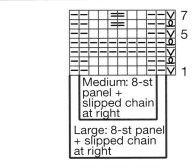

K/P CHART A
(OPTION 3 : NUPPS & LADDE RS)

Note: This pattern is worked over an odd number of rnds. Maintain slipped chain every other rnd.

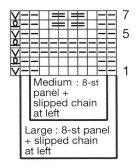

K/P CHART B
(OPTION 3 : NUPPS & LADDE RS)

Note: This pattern is worked over an odd number of rnds. Maintain slipped chain every other rnd.

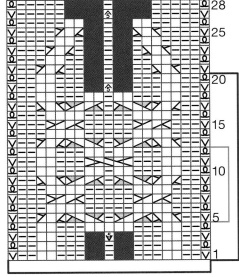

17-st panel, inc to 21 sts, dec to 13 sts

CENTER F RONT KNOT CHART

NOTES

Work 3 reps of Rows 1– 20.

First Rep: Work Rows 5 – 12 twice for double-knot. (total: 28 rnds)

2nd Rep: Work Rows 5 – 12 3 times for triple-knot. (total: 36 rnds)

3rd Rep: Work Rows 5 – 12 twice for double-knot. (total: 28 rnds)

To make leg shorter, work Rows 5 – 12 twice on 2nd rep.

To make leg longer, work [Rows 5 – 12] 3 times on First or 2nd Rep, or both.

After 3 reps are complete, work Rows 21 – 28, then work row 28 only until leg is desired length to heel.

Estonian Kapõtad Socks

Design by Nancy Bush

Kapõtad in the Kihnu dialect is a word for men's socks. *Kapõtad* came in either stripes or a single color. Men wore white socks for festival days and black or gray socks for work. Striped socks were a later fashion, worn for festival times rather than work. Women would knit *kapõtad* using stripe designs of their own choosing. Sometimes they would add a symbol or figure under the heel (it could be a family or farm mark) to indicate who owned the sock if it was lost. Today, this style of sock is popular on Kihnu and is even worn by women. I designed my own *kapõtad*, drawing from elements of several I have seen. I added a small eight-pointed star under the heel, to carry on the Kihnu tradition. Information for this design comes from *Elemõnu*, by Rosaali Karjam, text translated by Maret Tamjärv, with many thanks.

Size
Women's medium [US sizes 8–9]

Finished Measurements
Length from cuff to ankle: 8" [20.5cm]

Foot circumference: 8" [20.5cm]

Materials 🧵1
Helmi Vuorelma Oy (from Finland) *Satakieli* (fingering weight; 100% wool; 360yds [3290m] per 3½ oz [100g] skein): 1 skein Grey #901 (MC); ½ skein each Purple #582 (A), Blue #966 (B), Moss Green #985 (C), and Rust #288 (D)

Size 0 [2mm] double-pointed needles (set of 5) or size needed to obtain gauge

Stitch marker

Tapestry needle

Gauge
36 sts and 48 rnds = 4" [10cm] in St st (before blocking).

Adjust needle size as necessary to obtain correct gauge.

Pattern Notes
This sock is worked from the cuff down; there is a band of stripes on the heel flap and a star on the square heel turn; the toe is a pointed wedge toe.

This pattern is worked so there is a left and a right sock. Rounds begin at the inside instead of the back of leg so that the color changes occur at the inside of each leg.

Special Technique
Cross-Over Join: Join cast-on sts into a round as follows: slip the first cast-on st (at the point of the LH needle) onto the RH needle. With the LH needle, pick up the last cast-on st (which is now 1 st in from the end of the RH needle) and bring it up over the top of the previously moved st, placing it onto the point of the LH needle. In essence, the first and last cast-on sts have changed places and the last cast-on st surrounds the first.

Stitch Patterns

Stripe Pattern A (7 Rnds)

Work 1 rnd each in the following order: A, MC, C, B, C, MC, A.

Stripe Pattern B (7 Rnds)

Work 1 rnd each in the following order: B, MC, C, A, C, MC, B.

Patterns C and D, Star Motif

See charts.

Instructions

Cuff And Leg

With two needles held parallel and using a long-tail method and MC, CO 72 sts. Distribute sts evenly on 4 dpns; mark beg of rnd and join with a Cross-Over Join, taking care not to twist sts.

Work 22 rnds in K2, P2 Rib.

Knit 3 rnds.

Rnds 1–7: Work Stripe Pat A.

Rnds 8–14: With MC, knit 7 rnds.

Rnds 15–21: Work 7 rnds Stripe Pat B.

Rnds 22–28: With MC, knit 7 rnds.

Rnds 29–35: Work 7 rnds Stripe Pat A.

Rnds 36–42: With MC, knit 7 rnds.

Rnds 43–49: Work 7 rnds Pat C.

Rnds 50–56: With MC, knit 7 rnds.

Rnds 57–64: Work 8 rnds Pat D.

Heel Flap (Left Sock)

Note: Slip the edge sts where possible, as you add in new colors. If you find you are ready to begin a row and the color you need is on the other side, simply begin the row at the side where the color is attached, always keeping in St st.

Break MC. Slip next 37 sts onto 2 dpns to hold for instep.

Row 1 (RS): Join MC and knit across rem 35 heel sts.

Row 2: Sl 1, p34.

Row 3: Sl 1, k34.

Rep Rows 2 and 3 twice more.

Work 7 rows Stripe Pat C, slipping the edge sts where possible.

Work 20 rows St st with MC, slipping first st of each row, ending with a WS row. You should have approx 17 chains up each side of the flap.

Heel Flap (Right Sock)

Row 1 (RS): With MC, k35, turn. Slip rem 37 sts onto 2 dpns to hold for instep.

Beg with Row 2, complete flap as for Left Sock.

Turn Heel

Row 1 (RS): Sl 1, k22, ssk; turn, leaving rem sts unworked.

Row 2: *Sl 1, p12, p2tog.

Row 3: Sl 1, k12, ssk.

Row 4: Sl 1, work Star Motif across next 11 sts, p2tog.

Continue working Star Motif and turning heel until all side sts are in work—13 sts.

Gusset

Note: Pick up into the whole st as you work the sides of the heel flap, adjusting for the few rows where you might not have a slipped edge st. Read gusset instructions through because striping occurs while decreasing gusset.

Pick-up rnd: With needle holding heel sts (N1) and cont with MC, pick up and knit 17 sts along side of heel flap; N2 and N3: k37, keeping sts divided on 2 dpns; N4: pick up and knit 17 sts along side of heel flap, then k7 heel sts from N1; mark beg of rnd—84 sts with 23 sts on N1, 18 sts on N2, 19 sts on N3, and 24 sts on N4.

Rnd 2 (dec): N1: Work to last 3 sts, k2tog, k1; N2 and N3: knit across; N4: k1, ssk, knit to end—82 sts.

Rnd 3: Work even.

Rep [Rnds 2 and 3] 5 times—72 sts.

At the same time, on Rnd 8 (7 rnds of MC from Pat D on instep), beg Pat C; on Pat C Rnd 4, work 1A, *2D, 2A; rep from * around, ending with 1A.

Cont in pat, decreasing as necessary to complete gusset shaping.

Foot

Work even in est pat, working 7 rnds MC between alternating Pats D and C, ending having completed the second Pat D on the foot.

Knit 3 rnds with MC.

Toe

Adjust sts so you have 18 sts on each dpn.

Color pattern: Dec for toe following instructions below and at the same time, work 4 rnds with MC; work Pat C, then knit with MC to end.

Rnd 1 (dec): N1: Knit to last 2 sts, k2tog; N2: ssk, knit to end; N3 and N4: work as for N1 and N2—68 sts.

Rnd 2: Knit around.

Rep [Rnds 1 and 2] 8 times—36 sts.

Rep [Rnd 1] 7 times—8 sts.

Finishing

Break yarn, leaving a 6" [15cm] tail. Using tapestry needle, thread tail through rem sts, and pull tight. Weave in all ends. Wash gently and block on sock blockers or under a damp towel.

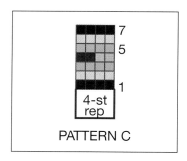

PATTERN C

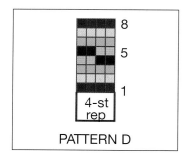

PATTERN D

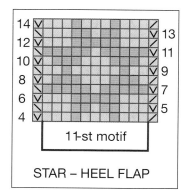

STAR – HEEL FLAP

COLOR AND STITCH KEY
☐ MC
■ A
■ B
☐ C
▨ D
☑ Sl 1
◪ P2tog on WS
◥ Ssk on RS

Bavarian Twisted
Stitches Socks

Design by Janel Laidman

Since the eighteenth century, knitters in the Austria/ Bavaria region have been using twisted stitches to adorn their garments, transforming this art form into a highly patterned style rich with texture and ornament. These stitch patterns were passed down from one generation to the next through the use of swatches as stitch libraries. Today, knitters around the world have access to these patterns and enjoy making these visually pleasing works of art.

Sizes
Women's small [US sizes 5–6] (medium [US sizes 7–9], large [US sizes 9–12]). Instructions are given for smallest size, with larger sizes in parentheses. When only 1 number is given, it applies to all sizes.

Finished Measurements
Foot circumference: 7½ (8½, 9½)" [19 (21.5, 24)cm]

Materials 🧶**1**🧶
Lorna's Laces *Shepherd Sock* (fingering weight; 80% superwash wool/20% nylon; 215yds [197m] per 2oz [56g] skein): 1 skein Firefly

Size 1 [2.25mm] double-pointed needles (set of 5) or size needed to obtain gauge

Cable needle

Tapestry needle

Gauge
32 sts and 44 rnds = 4" [10cm] in St st.

Adjust needle size as necessary to obtain correct gauge.

Pattern Notes
This sock is made from the cuff down, with a flap heel, gussets, and a wedge toe.

To change the size, change the stitch count by adding or removing purl stitches between the charts (revising stitch counts throughout pattern as necessary), or change the gauge by using a heavier/ lighter weight yarn or larger/smaller needles.

Crossed stitches are less elastic than other stitches. Try on your sock as you progress to make sure it is fitting and able to go over your heel. A snug fit in the ankle is normal.

Stitch Patterns

Rib (multiple of 4 sts)

Pattern rnd: *K2-tbl, p2; rep from * around.

Bavarian Patterns

See Charts A–E.

Eye Of Partridge

Row 1 (RS): *Sl 1, k1; rep from * across.

Row 2: *Sl 1, p1; rep from * across.

Rep Rows 1 and 2 for pat.

Instructions

Cuff

CO 64 (68, 72) sts. Distribute sts evenly across 4 dpns as follows: back of leg (N1 and N2): 32 (34, 36) sts and front of leg (N3 and N4): 32 (34, 36) sts. Mark beg of rnd and join, taking care not to twist your sts.

Work Rib pat for 6 rnds.

Leg

Set-up rnd: N1 and N2: work Chart C over 4 sts; Chart D over 6 sts, Chart E over 12 (14, 16) sts, Chart D over 6 sts, and Chart C over 4 sts; N3 and N4: work Chart A over 8 sts, Chart B over 16 (18, 20) sts, and Chart A over 8 sts.

Work even in est pats for 35 rnds—2 reps of charts are complete.

Heel Flap

Slip sts from N2 to N1 for heel; sts on other 2 dpns will remain on hold for instep.

Working back and forth on heel sts only, work Eye of Partridge pat for 30 rows.

Turn Heel

Row 1 (RS): K18 (18, 20), ssk, k1; turn.

Row 2: Sl 1, p5 (3, 5), p2tog, p1; turn.

Row 3: Sl 1, knit to 1 st before gap formed on previous row, ssk (1 st on each side of gap), k1; turn.

Row 4: Sl 1, purl to 1 st before gap formed on previous row, p2tog (1 st on each side of gap), p1; turn.

Rep [Rows 3 and 4] 4 (5, 5) times—1 st rem each side of heel.

Next row: Sl 1, knit to 1 st before gap, ssk; turn.

Next row: Sl 1, purl to 1 st before gap, p2tog; turn—18 (18, 20) sts on needle.

Gusset

Pick-up rnd: N1 (now heel/sole sts): Sl 1, knit across heel sts; with same dpn, pick up and knit 16 sts along side of heel flap; N2 and N3 (now instep sts): work Charts A, B, A as est; N4 (now heel/sole sts): pick up and knit 16 sts along other side of the heel flap, k9 (9, 10) sts from N1—82 (84, 88) sts with 50 (50, 52) heel/sole sts and 32 (34, 36) instep sts.

Rnd 1: N1: Knit to last 3 sts, k2tog, k1; N2 and N3: work Charts A, B, A as est; N4: k1, ssk, knit to end—80 (82, 86) sts.

Rnd 2: Work even.

Rep [Rnds 1 and 2] 8 (7, 7) times—64 (68, 72) sts with 32 (34, 36) sts each on instep and sole.

Foot

Work even in est pats until foot measures approx 2" [5cm] short of desired length.

Toe

Rnd 1: Knit around.

Rnd 2: *N1: Knit to last 3 sts, k2tog, k1; N2: k1, ssk, knit to end; rep from * on N3 and N4—60 (64, 68) sts.

Rep [Rnds 1 and 2] 9 (11, 11) times—24 (20, 24) sts with 6 (5, 6) sts per dpn.

With N4, knit across sts on N1; slip sts from N3 to N4—12 (10, 12) sts on each dpn.

Finishing

Cut yarn, leaving a 15" [38cm] tail. With tapestry needle and tail, graft toe closed using Kitchener st. Weave in ends. Block as desired.

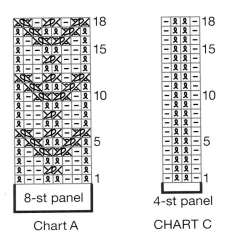

8-st panel

Chart A

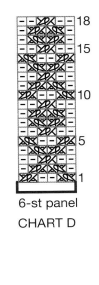

4-st panel

CHART C

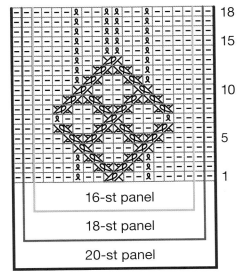

16-st panel

18-st panel

20-st panel

CHART B

6-st panel

CHART D

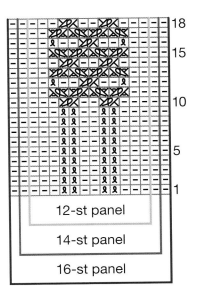

12-st panel

14-st panel

16-st panel

CHART E

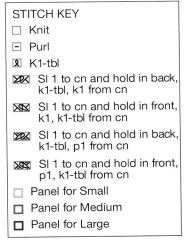

STITCH KEY

☐ Knit

⊟ Purl

K1-tbl

Sl 1 to cn and hold in back, k1-tbl, k1 from cn

Sl 1 to cn and hold in front, k1, k1-tbl from cn

Sl 1 to cn and hold in back, k1-tbl, p1 from cn

Sl 1 to cn and hold in front, p1, k1-tbl from cn

☐ Panel for Small

☐ Panel for Medium

☐ Panel for Large

Dura-Europos Socks

Design by Elanor Lynn

My interest in the history of textile arts led me to cross the globe as well as two millennia to revive this elegant leaf-and-ogee textile design. The results are remarkably similar to knitting. However, this older method is phenomenally tedious. I've managed to reproduce enough of this technique to understand how mind-numbing it can be to make a pair of socks in Dura-Europos patterns. These socks are a tribute to the hyper-developed skills of our ancestors, which would make our clumsy modern hands wilt.

Sizes

Women's small/medium [US sizes 6–8]

Sizing Options: To create a proportionally larger sock, work on larger needles. For a longer foot, work more plain rounds after the toe before beginning the stitch patterns on the foot. For a sock with a greater circumference, add 1 or 2 purl stitches between the Ogee and Leaf patterns.

Finished Measurements

Foot circumference: 7½" [19cm]

Foot length: 9" [23cm]

Materials 🧶❶🧶

Cascade Yarns *Heritage* (fingering weight; 75% wool/25% nylon; 437yds [400m] per 3½ oz [100g] skein): 2 skeins red #5607 **Note:** You will need only a small amount of the second skein, if at all.

Size 1 [2.25mm] double-pointed needles (set of 5)

Size 2 [2.75mm] double-pointed needles (set of 5) or size needed to obtain gauge

Size C/2 [2.75mm] crochet hook

Stitch marker

Tapestry needle

Gauge

40 sts and 50 rnds = 4" [10cm] in twisted St st (worked through the back loops) on larger needles.

Adjust needle size as necessary to obtain correct gauge.

Pattern Notes

This sock is worked from the toe up, with an increasing wedge toe, an increasing gusset, a short-row heel turn, and a heel flap joined to gusset stitches.

Working through the back loops: Every stitch, whether knitted or purled, is worked through the back loop (the few exceptions are noted in the pattern). To streamline the pattern, knit and purl stitches are assumed to be worked through the back loop, so if the pattern says "k1" or "p1," knit (or purl) the stitch through the back loop. Knitting through the back loop will create a severe amount of twist, especially on the sole.

Practice the stitch patterns in tandem so you are confident with how the rounds match up before starting your project.

Special Abbreviations

Inc1 (lifted knit-knit inc): Insert tip of RH needle kwise into the head of the st below the next st on the LH needle; transfer this new loop the LH needle and knit it; knit next st.

P1K1inc (lifted purl-knit inc): Insert tip of RH needle kwise into the head of the st below the next st on the LH needle; transfer this new loop the LH needle and purl it; knit next st.

K1P1inc (lifted knit-purl inc): Insert tip of RH needle kwise into the head of the st below the next st on the LH needle; transfer this new loop the LH needle and knit it; purl next st.

W&T (Wrap and Turn): Bring yarn to RS of work between needles, slip next st pwise to RH needle, bring yarn around this st to WS, slip st back to LH needle, turn work to begin working back in the other direction. **Note:** Wraps will not be "joined" on later rows.

Special Techniques

Provisional Cast-On: With crochet hook and waste yarn, make a chain several sts longer than desired cast-on. With knitting needle and project yarn, pick up indicated number of sts in the "bumps" on back of chain. When indicated in pattern, "unzip" the crochet chain to free live sts.

Decreases: The left-slanting decrease is worked k2tog-tbl. The right-slanting decrease is worked as k2tog, without working through the back loops.

Stitch Patterns

Leaf pattern (21-st panel, 16-rnd rep)

Ogee pattern (21-st panel; 32-rnd rep)

Inverted Leaf pattern (21-st panel; 16-rnd rep)

See charts.

Instructions

Toe

With smaller needles, using the provisional method, CO 21 sts.

Rows 1, 3, and 5 (RS): Knit, turn.

Rows 2, 4, and 6: Purl, turn.

Unzip the waste yarn from provisional cast-on and transfer 21 live sts to a 2nd dpn.

Pick-up rnd: N1: K11; N2: k10; pick up and knit 2 sts along side of rectangle; N3: pick up and knit 1 st along side of rectangle, k11 (*not tbl*); N4: k10 (*not tbl*), pick up and knit 2 sts along side rectangle, marking last st as beg of rnd; pick up and knit 1 more st and transfer to end of N1 (first st of next rnd)—48 sts, with 12 sts on each dpn.

Rnd 1: Change to larger needles; sl 1 (transferred st), knit around, working all sts tbl.

Rnd 2 (inc): N1: *K2, Inc1, knit to end; N2: knit to last 3 sts, Inc1, k3; rep from * on N3 and N4—52 sts with 13 on each dpn.

Rnd 3: Knit.

Rep [Rnds 2 and 3] 8 more times—84 sts with 21 sts on each dpn.

Knit 8 rnds.

Foot

Rnd 1 (set-up pats): N1: K1, k2tog-tbl, k6, P1K1inc (Leaf: left half); [p1, k1] 5 times, p1 (Ogee: right half); N2: [k1, p1] 5 times (Ogee, left half); K1P1inc, k6, k2tog, k2 (Leaf: right half); N3 and N4 (sole sts): k42.

Cont est pats through Rnd 48 (Leaf Rnd 16 and Ogee Rnd 16).

Begin Gusset

Cont with est pats and inc 2 sts every other rnd to create gusset as follows:

Rnd 1 (inc): N1 and N2: (instep): Cont in est pat; N3 and N4: (sole sts): Inc1, knit to last st, Inc1.

Rnd 2: Work even.

Rep [Rnds 1 and 2] 7 more times, ending with Leaf pat Rnd 16 and Ogee pat Rnd 32—100 sts distributed as 21-21-29-29.

Short-Row Heel Turn

Short rows will be worked in twisted St st on center 32 sole sts; other sts rem on hold for gusset and instep.

Set-up row (RS): N1 and N2: Work pats as est; N3: knit across; N4: knit to last 13 sts, W&T.

Row 2 (WS): P32; W&T.

Decreasing short rows

Row 3: Knit to 1 st before wrap on previous row; W&T.

Row 4: Purl to 1 st before wrap on previous row; W&T.

Rows 5-16: Rep [Rows 3 and 4] 6 times, ending with p18, W&T.

Increasing short rows

Row 17: K18; W&T. **Note:** There are now 2 wraps on the st.

Row 18: P18; W&T. **Note:** There are now 2 wraps on the st.

Row 19: Knit to double-wrapped st, k1 (double-wrapped st); W&T.

Row 20: Purl to double-wrapped st, p1 (double-wrapped st); W&T.

Rows 21–32: Rep [Rows 19 and 20] 6 times, ending with p32, W&T.

Work Heel Flap and Join to Gusset Stitches

Row 33 (RS): K32, k2tog-tbl (last wrapped st and next st), turn.

Row 34: P33, p2tog (last wrapped st and next st), turn.

Row 35: K1, [k1, sl 1] 16 times, k2tog-tbl, turn.

Row 36: Rep Row 34.

Rows 37–48: Rep [Rows 35 and 36] 7 times.

Row 49: K1, [k1, sl 1] 16 times, k2.

Row 50: P36.

Row 51: K2, [k1, sl 1] 16 times, k3.

Row 52: P38.

Row 53: K3, [k1, sl 1] 16 times, k4.

Row 54: P40

Row 55: K4, [k1, sl 1] 16 times, k5.

Row 56: N3: Work Rnd 1 of left half of Leaf pat over first 10 sts, work Rnd 1 of right half of Ogee pat over next 11 sts; N4: work Rnd 1 of left half of Ogee pat over first 10 sts; work right half of Leaf pat over last 11 sts. Do not turn.

Leg

Rnds 1–17: Cont est pats, with N1 and N3 working left half of Leaf pat and right half of Ogee pat and N2 and N4 working left half of Ogee pat and right half of Leaf pat, ending with Rnd 18 of Ogee pat and Rnd 2 of Leaf pat.

Next rnd (Ogee Rnd 19): Inc 4 sts around by omitting the p2tog decs and increasing as follows: P8, k1, Inc1, p1, Inc1, k1, p8—88 sts.

Cont in pat through Ogee Rnd 32, incorporating new sts into pat by purling 1 additional st at each edge of Ogee pat.

Inverted Leaf

Right sock: Replace Leaf pat with Inverted Leaf pat over N2 and N3, working left and right halves as before; work Leaf pat as est on N1 and N4.

Left sock: Replace Leaf pat with Inverted Leaf pat over N1 and N4; work est Leaf pat on N2 and N3.

Continue in pattern through Ogee pat Rnd 30; Inverted Leaf pat will work charted Rnds 1–16, then 3–18.

Next rnd: Work Leaf pat without incs or decs as follows: K7, p1, k5, p1, k7; work other pats as est.

Next rnd: Complete est pats.

Cuff

Change to smaller dpns.

Rnd 1 (dec): Work in P1, K1 Rib and dec 4 sts evenly around, maintaining rib—84 sts.

Rnds 2-15: Cont in est rib.

Rnd 16: *P1, yo, k1; rep from * around—126 sts.

Knitting the yo tbl, BO in est pat.

Finishing

Weave in all ends. Block to finished measurements.

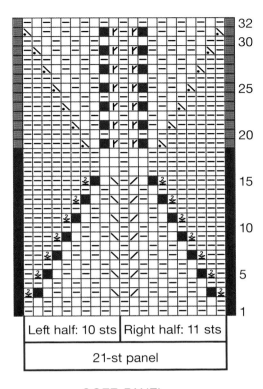

32
30

25

20

15

10

5

1

Left half: 10 sts | Right half: 11 sts

21-st panel

OGEE PANEL

STITCH KEY

□ K tbl

⊟ P tbl

■ No stitch

▨ No stitch until indicated in pat; p1-tbl after panel is increased.

☑ K2tog (not tbl)

◩ K2tog-tbl

◪ P2tog (not tbl)

⬚ Inc (lifted knit-knit inc)

⬚ P1K1Inc (a lifted inc)

⬚ K1P1Inc (a lifted inc)

⬚ Pfb

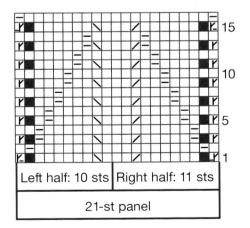

15

10

5

1

Left half: 10 sts | Right half: 11 sts

21-st panel

LEAF PATTERN

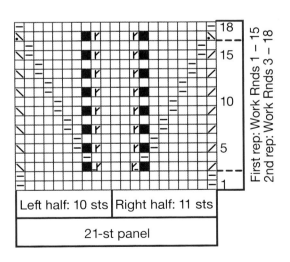

18

15

10

5

1

First rep: Work Rnds 1 – 15
2nd rep: Work Rnds 3 – 18

Left half: 10 sts | Right half: 11 sts

21-st panel

INVERTED LEAF

Andean-Inspired Socks

Design by Gretchen Funk

The knitting tradition of the people of the Andes Mountains is highly revered around the world. The region is perhaps best known for its *ch'ullu* hats (see page 115), characterized by either a riot of color or simpler patterns in more subdued, earthy tones. These cozy socks, inspired by the colorful designs found on the pages of *Andean Folk Knits*, by Marcia Lewandowski, combine a bright colorway on a more subdued, neutral ground. The drawstring at the top of the sock was modeled on the small colorful drawstring purses featured in *Andean Folk Knits*.

Sizes

Women's small [US sizes 6–8] (medium [US sizes 8–10], large [US sizes 9–12]). Instructions are given for the smallest size, with larger sizes in parentheses. When only one number is given, it applies to all sizes.

Finished Measurements

Length from cuff to ankle: 9 (10, 11)" [23 (25.5, 28)cm]

Circumference: 8 (8½, 9)" [20.5 (21.5, 23)cm]

Materials 🧶2 or 🧶3

Brown Sheep *Nature Spun Sport Weight* (sport weight; 100% wool; 184yds [168m] per 1¾ oz [50g] skein): 2 (3, 3) skeins Stone #701 (A); 1 skein each Storm #114 (B), Burnt Sienna #101 (C), Sunburst Gold #308 (D), Ash #720 (E), and Meadow Green #N56 (F)

Size 1 [2.25mm] needles for I-cord

Size 3 [3mm] double-pointed needles (set of 4) or a 40" [100cm] circular (for Magic Loop) or size to obtain gauge

Size 4 [3.5mm] double-pointed needles (set of 4) or a 40" [100cm] circular (for Magic Loop) or size needed to obtain gauge for colorwork

Stitch marker

Tapestry needle

Gauge

26 sts and 37 rnds = 4" [10cm] in St st using smaller needles and 2-color stranded St st using larger needles.

Adjust needle size as necessary to obtain correct gauge.

Pattern Notes

This sock is worked from the cuff down with a heel flap, gusset, and wedge toe.

Two-color stranded stockinette stitch tends to pull in more than 1-color stockinette stitch, so work color pattern with a larger set of needles to obtain gauge.

Slipped stitches are slipped purlwise unless specified as being slipped knitwise. Stitches on the heel flap are twisted by slipping them knitwise, thereby creating a denser fabric.

If using suggested yarn, gently hand-wash the socks to prevent felting.

Instructions

Cuff

With largest dpns and A, CO 52 (56, 60) sts.

Distribute sts evenly on 3 mid-size dpns; mark beg of rnd and join, being careful not to twist sts.

Rnds 1–4: Work K2, P2 Rib around.

Rnd 5: K2 (0, 2), p2 (0, 2), *k2, yo, p2tog; rep from * around.

Rnds 6-9: Work K2, P2 Rib around.

Leg

Next rnd: Change to largest dpns; knit and dec 2 (inc 4, --) sts evenly around—50 (60, 60) sts.

Knit 4 rnds.

Work 28 rnds following Chart.

Next rnd: Change to mid-size dpns; knit and inc 2 (dec 4, --) sts evenly around—52 (56, 60) sts.

With A, knit until leg measures 3½ (4, 4½)" [9 (10, 11.5)cm] from last colorwork rnd.

Heel Flap

Row 1 (RS): With 1 dpn and B, knit across first 16 (14, 18) sts, turn.

Row 2: Sl 1, purl across first 25 (27, 30) sts, turn. Sts on this needle are heel flap sts; redistribute rem 26 (28, 30) sts on 2 dpns and keep on hold for instep.

Row 3: Sl 1, *k1, sl 1 kwise; rep from * to last st, k1.

Row 4: Sl 1, purl to end.

Rep [Rows 1 and 2] 11 (12, 13) more times. Cut B.

Turn Heel

Row 1 (RS): Change to A; sl 1, k14 (16, 18) ssk, k1, turn.

Row 2 (WS): Sl 1, p5 (7, 9), p2tog, p1, turn.

Row 3: Sl 1, k6 (8, 10) ssk, k1, turn.

Row 4: Sl 1, p7 (9, 11), p2tog, p1, turn.

Cont working in this manner, working 1 more st on each row until all sts have been worked, ending with a WS row—16 (18, 20) sts

Gusset

Pick-up rnd: N1: Knit across heel sts, then pick up and knit 13 (14, 15) sts along the left edge of heel flap; N2: knit across instep sts; N3: pick up and knit 13 (14, 15) sts along the right edge of heel, k8 (9, 10) sts to center of heel—68 (74, 80) sts with 21 (23, 25) sts on N1 and N3 and 26 (28, 30) sts on N2.

Rnd 1: N1: Knit to last 3 sts, k2tog, k1; N2: knit; N3: k1, ssk, knit to end—66 (72, 78) sts.

Rnd 2: Knit around.

Rep [Rnds 1 and 2] 7 (8, 9) more times—52 (56, 60) sts, with 13 (14, 15) sts on N1 and N3.

Foot

Work even until foot measures 8 (9, 10)" [20.5 (23, 25.5)cm] from back of heel or 2" (2¼, 2½)" [5 (5.5, 6.5)cm] short of desired length. Cut A.

Toe

Rnd 1 (dec): N1: With B, knit to last 3 sts, k2tog, k1; N2: k1, ssk, knit to last 3 sts, k2tog, k1; N3: k1, ssk, knit to end—48 (52, 56) sts.

Rnd 2: Knit around.

Rep [Rnds 1 and 2] 9 (10, 11) times—12 sts rem.

Cut yarn, leaving a 12" [30.5cm] tail.

With tapestry needle and tail, graft toe closed using Kitchener st.

Finishing

Weave in all ends. Block socks.

I-Cord

With B and smallest dpns, CO 3 sts, leaving a 10" [25.5cm] tail.

*K3, do not turn, slip sts back to LH needle; rep from * until cord measures approx 20" [51cm]. Bind off.

Pull I-cord through the eyelets so the ends are at the center back of sock and covering the gap in the eyelets on small and large sizes.

Tassels

With several colors of project yarn, make 2 tassels about 2" [5cm] long. Secure to ends of I-cord.

COLOR KEY
■ A
■ B
▦ C
☐ D
☐ E
▨ F

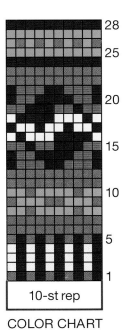

10-st rep

COLOR CHART

Poppy Socks: Turkish Socks

Design by Anna Zilboorg

This sock grows out of a traditional Turkish "hook" pattern (shown in the charts). It, in turn, developed from a motif used in rugs—as did most Turkish knitting patterns. The sock tradition in Turkey extends back to the very beginning of knitting and continued into the twentieth century, when it quickly began to decline. Complexly patterned and many-colored socks were an integral part of village life in Turkey for hundreds of years. Turkish socks, most often used as indoor slippers, were knit for special celebrations and given as gifts. This particular hook motif has appeared on wedding socks in horizontal bands of different colors, separated by bands of other patterns. Here the simple hooks change direction in the center front and center back of the sock. Each new repeat of the hook begins between the previous hooks on their last row. Both the figure and the ground are the same except where they change direction. I took this pattern from a book by Betsy Harrell called *Anatolian Knitting Designs* (Redhouse Press, 1981). It documents sock patterns from a knitting cooperative in Istanbul and provides information on the history and sociology of Turkish knitting. In that book, the pattern is knit in stripes of red and gold hooks on a black ground, which makes the pattern appear somewhat simpler than when it is worked in just two yarns. It is still surprising that something so conceptually simple becomes so visually complex and challenging to knit.

Size

Women's medium [US sizes 6–9]

Note: A larger sock can be made by using Socks that Rock medium weight (sport weight) and needles a size larger.

Finished Measurements

Length from top to ankle: 5" [12.5cm]

Foot circumference: 8" [20.5cm]

Materials 🧶1🧶

Blue Moon Fiber Arts *Socks that Rock Lightweight* (fingering weight; 100% superwash merino wool; 360yds [329m] per 4½ oz [127g] skein): 1 skein each Strange Brew (MC) and Muckity Muck (CC)

Size 2 [2.75mm] double-pointed needles (set of 5) or size needed to obtain gauge

Size 3 [3.25mm] double-pointed needles (set of 5) or size needed to obtain gauge

Stitch markers

Gauge

30 sts and 42 rows = 4" [10cm] in 1-color St st with smaller needles.

38 sts and 38 rows = 4" [10cm] in 2-color stranded St st with smaller needles.

32 sts and 35 rnds = 4" [10cm] in 2-color stranded St st with larger needles.

Adjust needle size as necessary to obtain correct gauge.

Pattern Notes

This sock is worked from the toe up. It begins with a short-row toe, followed by a patterned instep that is worked back and forth. The solid-colored sole and gusset are also worked back and forth while being joined to the instep at each edge. The heel is turned with short rows, then the gusset stitches are joined to the heel flap with decreases. The leg is worked in the round and is fully patterned.

When working the sole, add a second dpn when there are too many stitches for one dpn.

The two socks are different from each other. The first sock uses one color for the sole and cuff and the second sock uses the other. The patterning also reverses MC and CC for the second sock.

Special Abbreviation

W&T (Wrap and turn): Slip next st from the LH needle. Bring the yarn to the RS between needles. Return the slipped st to LH needle. Turn the work around, bring yarn to WS, and continue in the other direction.

Instructions

Toe

With smaller dpns and MC, using long-tail method, CO 31 sts.

Work decreasing short rows as follows:

Row 1 (WS): Sl 1, p28, W&T.

Row 2: K27, W&T.

Row 3: P26, W&T.

Row 4: K25, W&T.

Continue in this manner, working one fewer stitch before W&T on each succeeding row, until you have worked k9, W&T.

Work increasing short rows while working Toe Chart as follows:

Row 1 (WS): P10, W&T.

Row 2: K11, W&T.

Row 3: P12, W&T.

Row 4: K13, W&T.

Row 5: Join CC and beg patterning; p14, W&T.

Continue working 1 more st each row until all 31 sts are in work.

Instep

Row 1 (RS): Sl 1 with MC (background color), cont Instep Chart to last st, k1 with MC.

Cont working 40-row chart, slipping first st and working last st with MC on each row, repeating pat as necessary until instep measures 2″ [5cm] short of the desired length of the foot, ending with a purl row. (*Note last instep pat row worked; leg pat will begin with following row.*) Cut yarns.

Place a marker in the 15th slipped st from the last row on each side of the instep.

Sole

Using smaller needles, pick up (but do not knit) 31 sts along the toe cast-on, including 1 st from each side of the instep to get the full number.

Row 1 (WS): Join MC; sl 1, purl to last st, slip last st pwise; with RH needle, pick up next st on instep pwise; insert LH needle into back of 2 sts on RH needle and p2tog; turn.

Row 2: Sl 1, knit to last st, slip last st kwise; with RH needle, pick up next slipped st on instep kwise, insert LH needle into front of 2 sts on RH needle and k2tog; turn.

Continue in this manner until you reach the markers.

Gusset

Begin adding gusset sts.

Row 1 (WS): Sl 1, purl to end of row; pick up and purl under both legs of the slipped st on instep; turn— 32 sts.

Row 2: Sl 1, knit to end of row; pick up and knit under both legs of the slipped st on instep; turn—33 sts.

Rep [Rows 1 and 2] until all the slipped sts have been picked up—61 sole sts.

Turn Heel

Place markers 14 sts in from each end of sole. The heel will be turned on the central 33 sts.

Set-up row (WS): Sl 1, p13, sm, p31; W&T.

Row 1: K29; W&T.

Row 2: P28; W&T.

Continue in this manner, working 1 st fewer before working W&T on each succeeding row until you have worked k9, W&T.

Next row (WS): P9, *pick up next wrap and lay it over the st it wrapped, purl the st and wrap tog; rep from * to the last wrapped st; pick up last wrap as before and purl it tog with its st and the next st; turn.

Next row: Sl 1, knit across picking up the wraps and knitting them together with their sts; at the last wrapped st, pick up the wrap and knit it together with its st and the next st; turn—31 heel sts.

Heel Flap/Join Gusset

Row 1: Sl 1, purl to 1 st before gap left by turning on the last row, p2tog; turn.

Row 2: Sl 1, knit to 1 st before gap left by turning on the last row, ssk; turn.

Rep [Rows 1 and 2] until all 14 sts on the sides of the sole piece have been decreased—31 sts on needle. Cut yarn.

Leg

Mark center st of heel.

Shift the sts on the needles so that rnd begins 1 st after marked center heel and ends at the marked center heel st. Mark beg of rnd.

Work the Leg Chart around, beg with the pat row following the last row worked on the instep.

Work even, repeating the 40-rnd pat as necessary, until sock measures 4½" [11.5cm] from the end of the heel flap, or desired length of leg.

Cuff

Work K1-tbl, P1 Rib for 7 rnds.

BO very loosely, preferably with the tubular bind-off.

Second Sock

Work as for first sock, but reversing the colors. Weave in all ends. Block as necessary.

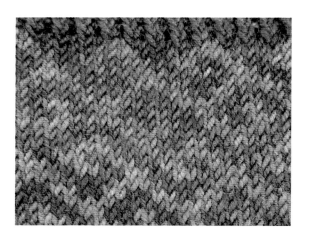

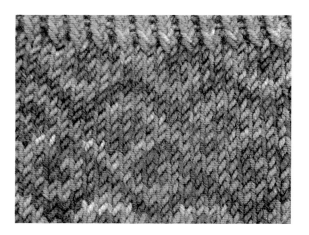

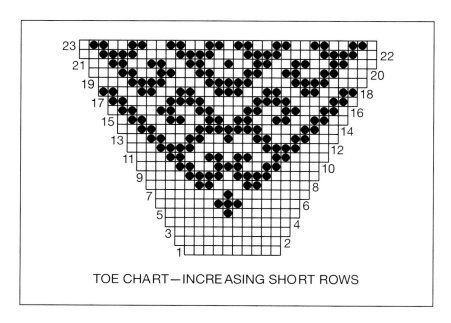

TOE CHART—INCREASING SHORT ROWS

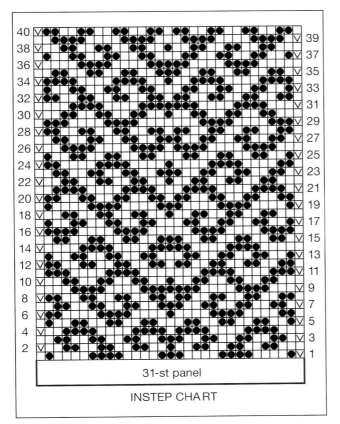

31-st panel

INSTEP CHART

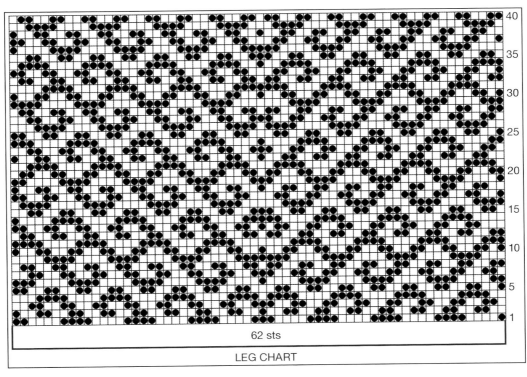

62 sts

LEG CHART

Abbreviations

beg   begin, beginning, begins

BO   bind off

CC   contrast color

cm   centimeter(s)

cn   cable needle

CO   cast on

cont   continue, continuing

dec(s)   decrease, decreasing, decreases

dpn   double-pointed needle(s)

est   establish, established

inc(s)   increase(s), increasing

k   knit

k1f&b   knit into front then back of same st (increase)

k1-tbl   knit 1 st through back loop

k2tog   knit 2 sts together (decrease)

kwise   knitwise (as if to knit)

LH   left-hand

MC   main color

mm   millimeter(s)

M1   make 1 (increase)

M1k   make 1 knitwise

M1p   make 1 purlwise

pat(s)   pattern(s)

p   purl

p1f&b   purl into front then back of same st (increase)

p1-tbl   purl 1 st through back loop

p2tog   purl 2 sts together (decrease)

pm   place marker

pwise   purlwise (as if to purl)

rem   remain(s), remaining

rep(s)   repeat(s), repeated, repeating

rnd(s)   round(s)

RH   right-hand

RS   right side (of work)

sc   single crochet

sk2p   slip 1 knitwise, k2tog, pass slipped st over

sl   slip, slipped, slipping

ssk   [slip 1 st knitwise] twice from left needle to right needle, insert left needle tip into fronts of both slipped sts, knit both sts together from this position (decrease)

ssp   [slip 1 st knitwise] twice from left needle to right needle, return both sts to left needle and purl both together through back loops

st(s)   stitch(es)

St st   stockinette stitch

tbl   through back loop

tog   together

w&t   wrap next stitch then turn work (often used in short rows)

WS   wrong side (of work)

wyib   with yarn in back

wyif   with yarn in front

yo   yarn over

*   repeat instructions from *

( )   alternate measurements and/or instructions

[ ]   instructions to be worked as a group a specified number of times

Standard Yarn Weight System

Categories of yarn, gauge ranges, and recommended needle and hook sizes

Yarn Weight Symbol & Category Names	1 Lace	2 Super Fine	3 Fine	4 Light	5 Medium	6 Bulky	7 Super Bulky
Type of Yarns in Category	Fingering, 10-count Crochet Thread	Sock, Fingering, Baby	Sport, Baby	DK, Light Worsted	Worsted, Afghan, Aran	Chunky, Craft, Rug	Bulky, Roving
Knit Gauge Range* in Stockinette Stitch to 4 inches	33–40** sts	27–32 sts	23–26 sts	21–24 sts	16–20 sts	12–15 sts	6–11 sts
Recommended Needle in Metric Size Range	1.5–2.25 mm	2.25–3.25 mm	3.25–3.75 mm	3.75–4.5 mm	4.5–5.5 mm	5.5–8 mm	8mm and larger
Recommended Needle U.S. Size Range	000 to 1	1 to 3	3 to 5	5 to 7	7 to 9	9 to 11	11 and larger
Crochet Gauge* Ranges in Signle Crochet to 4 inch	32–42 double crochets**	21–31 sts	16–20 sts	12–17 sts	11–14 sts	8–11 sts	5–9 sts
Recommended Hook in Metric Size Range	Steel*** 1.6–1.4mm Regular hook 2.25mm	2.25–3.5 mm	3.5–4.5 mm	4.5–5.5 mm	5.5–6.5 mm	6.5–9 mm	9mm and larger
Recommended Hook U.S. Size Range	Steel*** 6, 7, 8 Regular hook B–1	B–1 to E–4	E–4 to 7	7 to I–9	I–9 to K–10½	K–10½ to M–13	M–13 and larger

* GUIDELINES ONLY: The above reflect the most commonly used gauges and needle or hook sizes for specific yarn categories.

** Lace weight yarns are usually knitted or crocheted on larger needles and hooks to create lacy, openwork patterns. Accordingly, a gauge range is difficult to determine. Always follow the gauge stated in your pattern.

*** Steel crochet hooks are sized differently from regular hooks—the higher the number, the smaller the hook, which is reverse of regular hook sizing.

This downloadable symbol artwork is available at: YarnStandards.com.

Yarn Sources

Websites for the yarns used in the projects in this book are below. If you would like an alternate option for any yarn, or if a yarn has been discontinued, you can go to www.yarnsub.com to find options for substitution.

Berroco, Inc.
www.berroco.com

Bijou Basin Ranch
www.bijoubasinranch.com

Brown Sheep
www.brownsheep.com

Cascade Yarns
www.cascadeyarns.com

Frangipani
www.guernseywool.co.uk

Ístex
www.istex.is

Lorna's Laces
www.lornaslaces.net

Plymouth
www.plymouthyarn.com

Schoolhouse Press
www.schoolhousepress.com

Shibui Knits
www.shibuiknits.com

Stitch Diva Studios
www.stitchdiva.com

About the Designers

Dawn Brocco began her designing career working freelance for most of the major knitting publications. She has been self-publishing for the past thirteen years and now has more than one hundred patterns available. Her style embraces classic design with modern twists and whimsical design based on a love of nature. You can find Dawn Brocco Knitwear Designs at www.dawnbrocco.com and you can reach Dawn at dawn@dawnbrocco.com.

Elinor Brown lives with her husband, two kids, and two dogs in Columbus, Ohio, where she attends medical school at Ohio State University. Her knitting designs have appeared in *Interweave Knits*, *Knitscene*, *PopKnits*, *twist collective*, *Vogue Knitting*, and *Yarn Forward*. All can be found on Ravelry (www.ravelry.com/designers/elinor-brown), or on her blog, Exercise before Knitting (www.exercisebeforeknitting.com).

Beth Brown-Reinsel has been teaching knitting workshops nationally, as well as internationally, for more than twenty years. She wrote the book *Knitting Ganseys* and has recently filmed the DVD *Knitting Ganseys with Beth Brown-Reinsel*. Her articles have appeared in *Threads*; *Cast On*; *Interweave Knits*; *Shuttle, Spindle, Dyepot*; *Vogue Knitting*, and *Knitters* magazines. She continues to design for her own pattern line, available at www.knittingtraditions.com. Beth lives happily in Vermont.

Nancy Bush found her way to traditional knitting techniques and uses of ethnic patterns via a degree in art history and post-graduate studies in color design and weaving in San Francisco and Sweden. She has published articles and designs in *Knitters*, *Interweave Knits*, *Vogue Knitting*, and *Threads*. She has been the knitting contributor to *PieceWork Magazine* and is currently a member of the editorial advisory panel. She teaches workshops in the United States and abroad. She is the author of *Folk Socks* (1994), *Folk Knitting in Estonia*, (1999), *Knitting on the Road, Socks for the Traveling Knitter* (2001), *Knitting Vintage Socks* (2005), and *Knitted Lace of Estonia: Techniques, Patterns, and Traditions* (2008), all published by Interweave Press. She owns The Wooly West, a mail order yarn business in Salt Lake City, Utah.

Lily M. Chin is an internationally famous knitter and crocheter who has worked in the yarn industry for over 25 years as a designer, instructor, and author of books on knitting and crochet. She has created couture crochet for the New York Fashion Week runway collections of designers Ralph Lauren, Vera Wang, Diane von Furstenberg, and Isaac Mizrahi, and her work has been on the backs of celebrities and supermodels, from Raquel Welch and Vanna White to Cindy Crawford and Naomi Campbell. Learn more at www.lilychinsignaturecollection.com.

Donna Druchunas is the author of numerous books, including *Successful Lace Knitting: Celebrating the Work of Dorothy Reade*, *Ethnic Knitting Exploration: Lithuania, Iceland, and Ireland*, and *Arctic Lace: Knitted Projects and Stories Inspired by Alaska's Native Knitters*. She spent four months this year traveling in Europe to teach knitting workshops and do research for her next book, which will be about knitting in Lithuania. Visit her website at www.sheeptoshawl.com.

Teva Durham grew up in St. Louis, Missouri, with rather unconventional parents who had met in art school. As a teenager, Teva moved to New York City, attended the High School of Performing

Arts, and collected vintage clothing for costumes. Teva developed a particular fondness for sweaters culled from Lower Manhattan thrift shops and soon took up knitting. After pursuing acting and then journalism, Teva made a career out of her obsessive hobby and launched one of the first online knitting pattern sites, loop-d-loop.com, in 2000. She is the author of *Loop-d-Loop* (STC Craft, 2005) and *Loop-d-Loop Crochet* (STC Craft, 2007), and produces a line of yarns distributed by Tahki Stacy Charles.

Gretchen Funk lives and knits in Minnesota, where she and her husband own and operate the Triple Rock Social Club. She teaches knitting at The Yarnery in St. Paul and Crafty Planet, a needlework and craft shop in Minneapolis.

Chrissy Gardiner is a knitwear designer and teacher living in Portland, Oregon. She is the author of *Toe-Up! Patterns and Worksheets to Whip Your Sock Knitting into Shape* and the upcoming *Indie Socks*. She has also contributed designs to numerous books and magazines, and published her own pattern line. You can see more of her work at www.gardineryarnworks.com.

Anne Carroll Gilmour owned and operated Wildwest Woolies, a full-spectrum textile arts shop in Evanston, Wyoming, for nearly six years. She now lives in the beautiful Wasatch Mountains near Park City, Utah, where she works in her studio and also teaches workshops in spinning, weaving, and knitting. Her work has been featured in various textile publications and many galleries, museums, and private collections worldwide. Many of her knitwear patterns are available on her website: www.wildwestwoolies.com

Jennifer Hansen is the founder and chief designer of Stitch Diva Studios. She lives in Los Gatos, California, where she is a full-time crochet and knit designer, teacher, and writer. Her innovative crochet work has been featured in various books,

magazines, and television shows, including *Vogue Knitting*, *Interweave Crochet*, *The Happy Hooker*, *The Encyclopedia of Crochet*, and *Knitty Gritty*.

Janel Laidman has been obsessed with knitting since 1980, when she discovered that Danish girls could knit socks and learn physics at the same time. In the quest to reach the same lofty heights of coolness, she taught herself to knit too. Today Janel spends her time designing socks and other knitted garments, writing knitting books, feeding tulips to the deer, and knitting, of course! Janel is the author of *The Enchanted Sole: Legendary Socks for Adventurous Knitters*.

Melissa Leapman, a prolific designer, is the author of several bestselling knitting and crocheting books. Recent titles are *Hot Knits* and *Cool Crochet* (Watson-Guptill, 2004 and 2005), as well as the popular *Cables Untangled* and *Continuous Cables* (Potter Craft, 2006 and 2008). Her newest releases, *Color Knitting the Easy Way* and *Mastering Color Knitting*, were published in 2010. Her next book is due out in the Fall of 2011.

Elanor Lynn relocated from Brooklyn, New York, to Hollywood, California, three years ago. Since then, she's been knitting lots of palm trees into tapestries. She's currently exploring "handwritten" fonts in text-based work.

Hélène Magnússon is best known for her research around the traditional Icelandic intarsia that was seen in knitted inserts in shoes in Iceland in the past centuries. Her book, *Icelandic Knitting: Using Rose Patterns*, is available in three languages. She is a French native but a true Icelandic knitter, and has an Icelandic family. Find out more about her on her website: www.helenemagnusson.com.

Lucy Neatby, formerly a British Merchant Navy navigating officer, is now a full-time knitting designer, writer, and teacher. She loves all types of knitting, as long as they feature exuberant color work. As a teacher, she travels internationally and gets a kick from empowering knitters to take control of their stitches. To spread her message she filmed the sixteen-title Learn with Lucy DVD series and has written two books: *Cool Socks Warm Feet* and *Cool Knitters Finish in Style*.

Heather Ordover's latest joy has been writing and editing the first pattern book in the series *What Would Madame Defarge Knit? Creations Inspired by Classic Characters*. Prior to that, she spent her time writing and recording essays for *Cast-On: A Podcast for Knitters* and currently hosts her own long-running podcast, *CraftLit: A Podcast for Crafters Who Love Books* (think "audiobook with benefits"). Her crafty writing has appeared in *Spin-Off, WeaveZine*, and *The Arizona Daily Star*.

Kristin Spurkland learned to knit from her roommate, Sophie, in her freshman year of college. In 1998, she received her degree in apparel design from Bassist College in Portland, Oregon, and decided to pursue a career in knitwear design. She has been designing ever since. Kristin is the author of four books, including *The Knitting Man(ual)* (Ten Speed Press, 2007).

Pinpilan Wangsai was a massive failure when her grade-school teacher tried to teach her to crochet. After almost ten years of firmly believing she would never be able to make anything from yarn except pom poms, she tried again in college. Something clicked, and she went on to teach herself to knit almost anything by looking at books, Internet pages, and asking kind knitterly friends. She is now working as an elementary school teacher by day and knitting, spinning, or dreaming up new things by night.

Melissa Wehrle learned to knit from her grandmother when she was seven years old, but she quickly lost interest making Barbie tube dresses and put down the needles for several years. Her passion was renewed when she moved to New York City to study at the Fashion Institute of Technology, where she majored in fashion design and specialized in knitwear. Melissa graduated from FIT in May 2002 and has worked as a knitwear designer in the industry ever since. She is the junior/contemporary designer for a sweater manufacturer in New York City. In her free time, she designs for magazines, small yarn companies, and for her own line of handknit patterns called neoknits. She is also the creative director for One Planet Yarn and Fiber. Melissa's current projects and designs in progress can be viewed at her website, www.neoknits.com.

Anna Zilboorg took her love of yarn and knitting around the world and into the hills. The result has been countless knitting designs published in various magazines and a number of books, two of which feature sock designs: *Socks for Sandals and Clogs* and *Magnificent Mittens and Socks*. Anna is also the author of *Knitting for Anarchists*, a must-read for understanding how stitches are formed.

Index